Rabbits, Royalty and Religion
The agonies and ecstasies of an unlikely journalist

By John Alexander

Published by New Generation Publishing in 2014

Copyright © John Alexander 2014

First Edition

The author asserts the moral right under the Copyright, Designs and Patents Act 1988 to be identified as the author of this work.

All Rights reserved. No part of this publication may be reproduced, stored in a retrieval system or transmitted, in any form or by any means without the prior consent of the author, nor be otherwise circulated in any form of binding or cover other than that which it is published and without a similar condition being imposed on the subsequent purchaser.

www.newgeneration-publishing.com

New Generation Publishing

To: Henry, Ben, Millie, Lucy and Barnaby

Contents

Introduction 3
1 Dog fights over Bath 7
2 First taste of war 13
3 Back to school 20
4 At last---something to celebrate 25
5 Struggles of a cub reporter 33
6 Celebrities galore 40
7 Tackling the impossible 47
8 To Paris without love 55
9 Encounter with a Bluebell girl 64
10 Farewell to France 70
11 Menuhin, the Beatles and Princess Margaret 78
12 From the sublime to the ridiculous 90
13 In search of fresh pastures 97
14 And so to Cambridge 102
15 Let loose in Miami 109
16 A Square Deal? 114
17 Around the world in a plywood yacht 121
18 Training wannabe journalists 128
19 Disturbing the peace in Bexhill 134
20 Retreat into public relations 143
21 Born again---the first signs 150
22 Keeping Sunday Special 158
23 Parliament under a banyan tree 164
24 St Peter in the Pub 170
Appendix 176

Introduction

'No kidding, we're being attacked by a UFO.' The shrill voice of an excited, slightly inebriated teenager is not what you want to hear at three in the morning, not when sleep after a hellish day in an undermanned newsroom can be such a precious commodity 'Who put you up to this?' I screamed, trying to identify which junior reporter under my tutelage would have the nerve to disturb me at such an unearthly hour.

Through the haze of semi consciousness, I tried to make it clear to the caller that his already fragile employment status was now seriously jeopardised so he might as well risk all and conclude whatever little caper he and his pals had dreamed up after too many pints of ale in the Burleigh Arms.

With trembling voice, the would-be journalist tried very hard to tell me he had not made the call to annoy me but something very dramatic and out-of-the-ordinary was happening in the city.

'Come off it Jeremy (it is Jeremy isn't it?) if you want to wind me up couldn't you choose something more original than Unidentified Flying Objects.' Trying to control my temper, I stressed that no one above the mental age of seven gave any credence to visitors from outer space and anyway if little green men had decided to invade Cambridge's prestigious colleges, the burly gate porters trained to cope with marauding students would have no difficulty in keeping them at bay 'til morning.

Now fully awake, this was the flippant response Jeremy got for his trouble but as I was about to end the call with a furious goodbye, I remembered that Jeremy was not the sort of young man who could be dragged easily into a silly stunt of this nature. Not a brilliant prospect certainly, but serious enough in his ambitions not to damage his fledgling journalistic career by disturbing one of his seniors at an unearthly hour.

And to his credit he did not give up. 'There's a trail of damage through the city centre and beyond,' he reported with growing excitement, 'tiles are strewn everywhere and whatever it is has attacked one of the college buildings. People are talking about being disturbed in the early hours by a swishing sound outside their bedroom windows. Some of the people I talked to were really frightened.'

'Calm down,' I said, 'it's just a freak storm; happens in other countries all the time.'

'Don't think so,' my eager young colleague retorted, 'no rain, no wind, no thunder, no lightning and the moon is shining. The weather can't be the cause.'

With little prospect of getting back to sleep, I decided reluctantly to join Jeremy at the spot where 'the attack' had allegedly started. The sound of fire engines and police cars moving around in the distance convinced me that something out of the ordinary might be happening.

I didn't have to travel far to realise Jeremy was not exaggerating about the agitation of many residents who despite the unfriendly hour were outside their homes speculating with neighbours about the identity of the night visitor. In the moonlight, it was quite possible to plot a course towards the city centre. Whatever had been skimming the rooftops had deposited a trail of tiles and toppled pieces of street furniture.

We kept walking and didn't stop until confronted by what to the imaginative eye might well have seemed like a UFO of considerable dimensions. The moonlight shining on its silvery exterior created a spine-tingling vision, not unlike a Dr Who creation. Rhythmic metal sounds heard nearly half a mile away, added to the feeling that Cambridge was playing host to some very strange visitors indeed.

Bravely, we advanced (bravely because we carried nothing to defend ourselves) and gradually in the first rays of dawn it became obvious this was not something which had defied earth's gravitational pull. 'I don't believe it, it's a barrage balloon, what in the hell is it doing there?'

'Don't ask me' said a bewildered Jeremy, who had probably never seen a barrage balloon at close quarters in his life. To be honest neither had I, since my acquaintance with these ugly, unwieldy contraptions went back quite a few years when Britain was fending off repeated attacks from the air during the Second World War. This slowly deflating balloon, which had dragged 2,000ft of heavy metal cables across Cambridge's rooftops, had broken loose from its moorings at R.A.F. Cardington, Bedfordshire and had come to rest when its cables wrapped around scaffolding on a building site in the grounds of St John's College.

Twisting like a corkscrew, the cable had also struck a building occupied by students. When we arrived on the scene one occupant was standing by a pile of bricks telling a small crowd gathered around him that he was asleep at the top of the block when he was disturbed by a catastrophic noise. 'I saw a piece of heavy cable twisting around outside my window, then heard pieces of the building clattering to the ground.'

'How are they going to get that down?' asked Jeremy, who could see that although the balloon was hovering barely above church spire height, considerable damage to other historic buildings could be caused if the operation was handled clumsily. It was something which could not be done in a hurry especially as the balloon still contained a considerable volume of hydrogen.

Knowing that back at the office they would be waiting for a first edition account of what had given citizens the fright of their lives, I told Jeremy to go, write up his story and then get some sleep. 'I'll stay here and see how they manage to bring this monster under control,' I offered. 'You deserve the by-line, Jeremy; perhaps you'll make a journalist after all.'

As the sun appeared over the top of Cambridge's skyline, I made myself as comfortable as I could on a piece of grass and resigned myself to a long wait. There was talk of needing special equipment which had to travel some distance. It began to look as if the city would have to live with its unwanted floating visitor for some time.

***

1

Dog Fights over Bath

When was the last time I lay sprawled on grass looking at a barrage balloon? Not one balloon, as I remembered, but a cluster hovering over the hills of the West Country. We could see them in the distance protecting, the grown-ups told us, Bristol and important ports such as Avonmouth. Our historic city of Bath was not considered to be a German target so it didn't get even one barrage balloon. I heard my father telling a neighbour that they were a bit of a nuisance because they were as much of a danger to our fighters as they were to the German bombers.

Like most six-year-olds, I was without fear and watched with fascination what was happening in the skies above our modest terrace house in Brunswick Street. I had been the first to notice the balloons and pestered my parents for an explanation. They knew I was aware of the war with Germany and that some of the aeroplanes passing overhead were not ours. On a couple of particularly exciting days I had actually witnessed smaller, faster planes chasing the bigger ones and one boy at school had brought in a piece of metal which he claimed was the empty case of a tracer bullet which had fallen to the ground. The teacher snatched it from his grasp and threw it some way out of a window. We decided he was afraid it might explode and injure us.

My parents knew little about the dangers we were facing until Dad was ordered to join the National Fire Brigade. Then, he was able to tell us, the balloons were hoisted into the air in the hope enemy planes might bump into them and come crashing to earth.

In moments of contemplation lying on the lawn, I wondered what would happen if a plane-full of bombs came down on our garden. Presumably, there wouldn't be much left of Brunswick Street and we would be blown into little bits, too. Dad tried to assure us that if a German plane did come down it would be some distance away from our home. I was not so sure.

During one of my day dreaming periods, a much loved uncle, Uncle Tom, walked into the garden carrying an interesting package. He was one of the really cheerful members of our family and always referred to me as 'my boy'. He rarely visited without bringing something to fire my interest. Fire was the right word on this occasion because when I had pulled off the packaging there was a fireman's outfit complete with helmet, hatchet, whistle and an impressive identification badge to tell everyone I was an important person to have around when there was an emergency. I donned the gear, grabbed the end of the watering hose and danced around the garden, letting out whoops of joy. Running up to Uncle Tom for the umpteenth time I said it was great fun but it would be better if I had a fire to put out.

'Hang on a minute and we'll do something about that,' said Uncle Tom who had been busy stuffing a pile of old newspapers into our metal dustbin. My eyes opened wide as he took out a box of Bryant and May matches. Surely he was not going to...yes he was! 'Mummy won't like it if her dustbin gets burnt,' I protested.

'Mummy won't like it if her little boy gets hurt,' said Mum as she stepped into the garden waving a duster and giving poor old Uncle Tom some menacing looks.

'Don't worry, Vi,' he said. 'I won't let him stand too close. He can spray his hose from yards away.'

Mum was not happy but she could see cousin Tom was taking care and it would be no bad thing if the maggots, regular visitors to her dustbin in the summer months, got their deserts. It was a happy memory. Fireman John, just like his Dad, tackling a fire that threatened the whole neighbourhood. The water from the hose did its job rather too quickly for my liking, two squirts and the newspaper was reduced to a small pile of charcoal. The fate of the maggots was not something a six-year-old was going to worry about.

Tom was still being scolded by Mum, when Dad appeared in the garden wearing his fire brigade uniform, hated by him but adored by me. He had just come off duty and he didn't seem to know whether to be cross or amused by the scene in front of him. Obviously no harm had been done, not even to the dustbin, so with a smile on his face he gave Tom a mock punch on the chin and me a friendly hug.

'So your uncle's been up to his tricks again, has he? What will he think of next?' Dad's words were partially blurred by a sound that was becoming more and more familiar as the days passed by.... the distant roar of heavy aircraft heading for a new target, probably Avonmouth Docks the destruction of which, I was told, would be considered a valuable contribution to the German war effort. I was becoming more and more aware that terrible things were happening in other parts of the country but my young mind would not absorb the possibility that perhaps the city we lived in would actually be subjected to a deliberate attack.

I was about to find out how wrong I was. Dad dragged from behind his comfortable desk to serve the country on the home front---he was one of the few with business responsibilities considered important enough to excuse him from full military duty---was never going to enjoy the rigorous training necessary for even part-time firemen. Overweight and unfit initially, he still had to be capable of climbing a ladder to carry a smoke affected casualty to safety. It took weeks to get him into shape and Dad started to think it might have been better to join the Army and get a cushy posting somewhere in the African desert. Of course, he later realised there were no comfortable postings anywhere during the period of the Second World War.

Dad, Mum and Uncle Tom went into a little huddle and the serious tone of their voices made me realise that my game in the garden had been forgotten and there was something afoot they didn't want me to know too much about. Maybe I was only six, but before the week was out I was to be made aware of the terrors of war and what lengths one country would go to, to crush and demoralise another.

Until this point my childish view of what was happening did not go beyond the simple fact that England was being attacked by a country on the other side of the English Channel and I had little understanding of where Germany came into the picture.

For most children of my age everything happening in 1942 was a bit of an adventure. We had been issued with gas masks which we hated putting on but managed to turn into a joke by pulling funny faces at each other through the Perspex eye piece. Some of my friends spoke of the digging their family was doing in the back garden to provide an air-raid shelter and we had strict instructions about what do when the creepy sirens wailed their message of warning over the rooftops.

A sound sleeper, I didn't hear the ear-piercing warnings but my sister, Ann, who loved to demonstrate how grown up she was, liked to recount how she joined Mum and Dad, in their bed where they listened to the bombers making their way to more important targets than quaint little Bath. Obviously, they had overlooked the Admiralty offices in the centre of the city and the secrets kept there.

He didn't tell us openly but later we discovered that Dad had been given information that the Germans were planning a series of raids on Britain's historic towns and cities in reprisal for the damage the RAF had inflicted on some cherished buildings in Lubeck and Rostock. They were later to be dubbed the 'Baedaeker' raids because the target towns and been selected from the Baedaeker tourist guide to Britain.

'What was the point of both sides killing ordinary people?' I remember asking my father only to get a rebuke from my sister that I was too young to understand. Dad didn't believe Bath would suffer but said we should take precautions 'just in case.' He would be on duty but our instructions were to head for the cellar if the sirens went off that night. The cellar was a nasty little cavern partially beneath the road, where the household supplies of coal were stored. I hated it because the cat used it as the place to do its business and it always smelt horrible. Plus the fact that there were no windows and if the house collapsed the few stairs leading out of the cellar would almost certainly be blocked by debris. From what I had overheard listening to the adults, that was probably what would happen. I shuddered at the prospect of being buried alive in that horrible cellar

Mum decided it was better to be safe than sorry. To the cellar we would have to go if the siren went that night. With Ann's help she decided to make an effort, feeble as it was bound to be, to make the cellar more habitable. The coal dust was swept as far as it would go into the farthest corners and a couple of chairs were installed along with a garden lounger which would be my bed in the event of an attack.

As usual, I didn't hear the siren and protested loudly when Mum started to haul me out of bed. 'We're not staying up here tonight, young man,' she said as she wrapped a blanket around me and headed for the stairs. Ann was already on her way, calling to us to 'hurry up.' She was obviously a lot more worried than I was. In the cellar, the one small light bulb was already flickering ominously, making us think that some sort of attack had started and electricity supplies were being threatened.

Mum tried to keep us calm by recalling that on previous nights the all-clear siren brought early relief as the German bombers continued their journey to places they considered more important. Bristol had been the nearest target so far and I had overheard my parents talking about friends who had survived but had been terrified out of their wits. Dad's newspaper office was right in the centre of it all but somehow the building in Silver Street escaped serious damage. His fire brigade duties and concern for his family meant he had more on his mind at this time than circulating a newspaper.

2

First Taste of War

There was no all-clear siren that night. Instead, we had a taste of warfare right on our doorstep although I had to admit that even the first too-close-for-comfort explosions didn't disturb me as I had fallen asleep quite quickly in the canvas garden lounger. What did disturb me was a broomstick flying across the cellar and landing on my improvised bed. With a short sharp scream I sat up and was greeted by the sight of my mother and sister clutching each other amid a cloud of black dust. Household utensils that had occupied a place on a wall rack were lying on the floor, apart from the brush which had headed in my direction.

There was a look of terror on the faces of my mother and sister and I quickly joined them in a huddle. I think we were all expecting the next bomb to land on Brunswick Street but nobody spoke until after what seemed like a thousand years the all-clear siren sounded. Cautiously we returned to the upstairs room, to find no serious damage just a few ornaments and photo frames lying on the floor.

Our hope was that once the immediate danger had passed they would allow Dad off duty to check on his family and we were rewarded by the sound of his reliable little Morris 8 making the steep ascent between a row of houses, definitely not built with the motor car in mind. The road was so narrow his practice was to reverse the entire length of it so that the vehicle was facing in the right direction when duty called.

'Are you all OK,' he inquired as he came through the front door and we gave him feeble assurances. 'You were all in the cellar, I hope,' he said heading for the short flight of stairs leading to the bottom of the house. 'Good God, did these brushes and things fall or did you take them down?' he inquired,

'An explosion blew them off the wall,' Mum told him, 'how far away did that bomb fall?'

Dad explained it had landed on a garden nursery less than half a mile away but it was not thought to be part of an organised raid. 'Probably the German pilot had one deadly missile left in his bomb carriage and decided to get rid of it as he headed for home.'

If there was nothing particularly reassuring about this piece of news, then the next bit was positively alarming. 'We've been told Bath is on the German reprisal list and there is a chance all hell will break loose again tonight.'

'What's a reprisal?' I started to ask but immediately realised I was not going to get a quick answer.

'Steady on,' Mum urged, 'you'll frighten the kids to death. But it was too late Ann and I had been listening and even if I was too wet behind the ears to understand what Dad was saying, Ann certainly wasn't. She took my hand and told me not to worry. But there were not many living in Bath that day who were not terrified about what might happen during the 48 hours ahead. The 'Baedaeker' raids theory had been in common circulation for some time despite attempts by the Government to keep the information under wraps.

Something I never fathomed was how, if bombing raids on Bath were thought to be imminent, Dad managed to be off duty on that day of death and destruction, April 25, 1942. We later learned that men with young families were given the chance to stay at home and report for duty if the worst happened. Even local officials were in denial about the seriousness of a raid on the West Country's most beautiful cities. It just won't happen, some of them insisted

Anyway, what I do remember was my father's determination not to allow us to stay in Brunswick Street that night. Still waving a broom handle in a manner which suggested he might be about to mount a single-handed attack on the enemy, he announced that under no circumstances were we going to suffer a second night sitting in the cellar, terrified and expecting the next bomb to have our name written on it. I was allowed to play in the garden while the car was filled with blankets, pillows, flasks of tea, jam sandwiches, fruit and biscuits. Mum was worried about her own mother and stepfather who ran a small motor accessories shop right in the centre of the city. Dad had called on them but they were quite determined to stay put because they, too, had a cellar which they were convinced would protect them from falling debris.

The days were getting longer but it was almost dark as Dad checked the windows of the house, made sure the front and back doors were locked and started to bundle us into the car. 'I'll have to remove some of this stuff if we are all to get in,' he declared, but he was not taking his wife's dexterity into account. As she shuttled things around thrusting bottles into places where there simply wasn't any apparent space, she told us to pull our legs up to our chins if we had to. It would be an uncomfortable ride but we were glad to be going somewhere where the Germans couldn't get at us. Or so we thought.

Bath is surrounded by hills and I stayed awake long enough to sense that Dad was heading outwards and upwards. This is where I have to start relying to some extent on the testimony of my sister and parents because despite being trussed like a chicken prepared for the oven, I fell asleep.

It was not a nice experience waking up. It was not so much the noise, although that was horrible, but the extraordinary red glow that seemed to fill the entire windscreen and infiltrate every corner of the car. We were on a plateau high above the city which I recognised immediately as our favourite spot for games of family cricket. We were often joined by uncles and cousins on Bannerdown for a picnic and a battle with bat and ball.

'What's happening?' was my feeble little question and for a while no one answered. Mum and Dad were just staring straight ahead and Ann had her arm around her mother and although fascinated was trying not to look in the direction of the city.

'How can they possibly be alive in the middle of all that,' I heard my mother say, 'the city is an inferno and they live right in the middle.'

'They'll be all right in their cellar,' my father said but even I noticed he didn't say this with much conviction.

'When will we be able to go down? I'll have to go and see for myself,' said Mum.

'Not while those fires are raging, you won't. We'll wait an hour. I doubt whether the wardens will allow us through, anyway.'

'Will you have to go back to the station?'

'Of course, I will. I should be there now but we'll make sure we've still got a home. Then if things have simmered down, I'll report for duty.'

There was no going back to sleep so I kept pestering Dad to drive down the hill and head for home. Boy-like, I was thinking about my toys, particularly my railway set, but being only six I suppose I could be forgiven for not understanding the extent of the death and destruction all around us. Eventually Dad rolled the car slowly down the hill---the shortage of petrol meant he never started the engine until he had to---and made for the garage we used half-a-mile or so from Brunswick Street. There was not much garage left but enough room on the forecourt to leave the car.

If early parts of my story are tainted, not so much by memory loss as by the ease with which a six year old can fall asleep even under the most extreme circumstances, then the next six minutes of my young life can be recalled today as though they had happened a few months ago.

My father wrapped a blanket around me and started the long trudge along the London Road and then turned into the bottom of our street. As he walked past the homes of our neighbours all I could hear was the crunch of broken glass. 'All the windows are gone,' said Ann, 'and all the tiles.' Eyes now wide open with fear, I did notice that the walls and roofs were still intact but there was another shock as we approached our front door. It wasn't there any longer; it had been blown off its hinges.

My mother walked through the gaping hole and re-emerged wiping tears from her face. 'It's terrible, most of the plaster on the walls is now on the carpets; and to think I had just finished the spring cleaning.' My Dad put his arm around her to console her but the tears kept coming. Later he told us that a massive bomb had fallen on allotments behind our house and it was the blast that did all the damage.

'I'm just thankful I got you to a safe place last night. If I hadn't I think you would have all died of fright.'

The number of people who perished in Bath on those two nights of horror was not something discussed with a six-year-old but even at that age I soon became aware that our family doctor, Dr Mary Middlemas, was no longer with us. She was killed when a bomb struck her house in the fine row of Georgian buildings known as The Paragon.

It was several years before I became aware of the full extent of the death and destruction---417 dead, 357 seriously injured, 515 slightly wounded. Over 200 buildings of architectural or historic interest were destroyed, yet amazingly the Bath Blitz remains a mere footnote in the many accounts of Britain at war.

***

Although of tender years, the dreadfulness of the destruction and the death-toll punched into my brain a host of memories that can still form part of a nightmare. I was told that my grandparents had survived and their small motor accessories shop was still intact but it was sometime before I was taken to Chapel Row to see for myself. We had to drive through Queen Square and that was the first time I could see for myself what a bomb was capable of doing if it directly hit a building. The Francis Hotel, or most of it, was gone.

Grandma Lilley and Grandpa Little, as we called them, were surprisingly cheerful as they described how they cheated the bombs by retreating to their cellar. They didn't describe in detail the fear they must have felt when an entire area of the city, known as Kingsmead was completely wiped off the map. Grandpa talked about it in his usual casual manner: 'The bombs fell within spitting distance of the back garden', I recall him telling us, 'but if they were after your Gran and me it just shows what lousy shots they were.'

There were many who were not so fortunate that night. One extraordinary account was later put together by *Martin Wainwright,* an Oxford University student who wrote a regular column in the Bath Evening

Chronicle. His booklet '*The Bath Blitz*' pointed out that few memorials or plaques remained and most visitors left Bath without any idea of what happened in 1942. That is unless they discovered Haycombe Cemetery where young children still ask their parents: 'What are all those little crosses for?' They learn that they are standing on the spot where three communal burial services were held and there was no opportunity to be particular about who went into which grave.

Martin Wainwright's book was passed on to at least two of my grandchildren when their teachers asked them, as part of a project, to question older members of their families about 'what happened during the war.'

It was a pity Wainwright's account didn't get wider circulation. Here is one extract in his well researched account: '*The toll in Bath was higher than in any of the other towns attacked by the Baedaeker raiders. Bath's dead formed a major proportion of the 938 killed by air attacks on Britain during April when Exeter, Norwich and York were also targeted. Cellars and the broad open stairwells of the city's older homes saved a great many lives. A young girl was trapped in a cupboard in a house where a bomb killed 14. She was stuck beneath the rubble for three days while rescuers dug. As the scraping of the shovels grew louder, she started to tap with a spoon. The diggers heard the small plea for help and the girl was saved. From another pile of wreckage a nine-year-old boy burrowed his own way out.*'

3

Back to School

It was years later after reading Wainwright's booklet that I realised how close several members of the Alexander family were to near-death situations.

While Brunswick Street was being repaired my sister and I were shipped out to relatives with instructions to get back to school as soon as possible. My first school was St Saviour's, Larkhall, and across the road, my great grandfather, a wonderful man in his 80s, kept house for himself and his two spinster daughters, one a teacher in the school, the other a seamstress who ruled a group of young women at Jolly's, a 'posh' shop in Milsom Street, with a rod of iron. A frequent customer was Queen Mary who had escaped the chaos of London and moved to the West Country to live at Badminton; so frequent were her visits, the store provided her with her own toilet and rest room. Aunt Eleanor may have seemed like a bit of a dragon to her team of budding tailoresses but to us she was 'Dobbin', a nick name derived from the fact that she was willing to get down on her hands and knees and give us donkey rides around the lounge. Her 'young ladies' at Jolly's would no doubt have found this a very strange sight indeed.

Her sister, Fanny, very prim and proper but a good teacher, rightly kept Ann and I at arm's length and left her father to spoil us. This he did with great joy because it was to his house in Brooklease Buildings that a group of us marched from St Saviour's during air raids. He had a cellar which was considered safer than any of the school accommodation and we boys approved because he kept his stock of apples just outside the cellar. His fruit supplies quickly dwindled but he didn't mind. He loved our frequent visits.

Food rationing meant we children never saw a banana and our allocation of sweets was pitiful. Milk was delivered to the schools in crates, a practice that continued long after the war had ended. Uncle Tom and other older members of the family worked at Stotherts and Pitt which was targeted by the German bombers because instead of its usual output of cranes and other heavy lifting gear, it produced tank and torpedo parts. Almost everyone walked to their workplace and this meant a three-mile hike for those members of the Larkhall clan who made their living at the world renowned engineering works.

These hard-working members of the family used to get very hungry and in such dire times it was not easy to find food that would fill their bellies and keep up their strength. When Mum talked about her courting days before the war she always recounted with a look of disgust on her face how they all loved pork...very fatty pork. Just to look at it made her feel sick but it did marvels for men who walked long distances to carry out very heavy and exhausting tasks. *Wainwright* recalled how on the first raid the Germans followed the moonlit Avon and aimed their bombs at the engineering works. A tank was hurled into the river and an armoured car turned turtle in a bombed-out shed. Almost immediately wires and poles came down and communications were destroyed. Messengers pedalled out on cycles but even they became useless as a sea of shattered glass continually punctured their tyres.

Eventually Brunswick Street was returned to a reasonable state of repair and having gone back to live there, Ann would take me on what seemed a long walk along the London Road and into Larkhall. I probably didn't appreciate it much in those days but we always passed the graceful St Savour's Church, where all the Alexander family services were held. Mum and Dad married there in the late 1920s but only a few close friends and relatives knew why Mum was moving down the aisle with a jerky limp. While in her early twenties a serious operation to her thyroid had gone wrong, sending poison to one of her hips. She never played tennis or danced again but because she never talked about her handicap or the way it affected her life, we kids just accepted it as the norm. She was a tiny woman but a tough, loving mother and a wonderful manager of family affairs. Dad used to admire her ability to handle the family finances and regularly told us: 'When it comes to saving follow your Mum's example. I always know that if I give her just 10 pennies she'll save five of them.'

They met while working for the Bath Chronicle, a local newspaper of record which was to have an important impact on my life in future years. Dad was on the business side of the operation but Mum had a job that could only have been on offer in days when communications relied on something one step ahead of pigeon-post. She was responsible for getting the racing results in the stop press and did this by using nothing as modern as a teleprinter or fax, rather a system more familiar to sailors on the high seas...the morse code. Probably, a large percentage of readers never advanced further than the back page. All they wanted to know was the name of the winning nag in the 2.30pm at Cheltenham.

There never was another air raid on Bath but the local firemen, praised for their gruelling and distressing task of searching for survivors and bodies in the ruins, were kept on duty until the end of the war. And it was not only the firemen who worked night and day. Wardens who had been out on the streets checking shelters and cellars continued their nightly watch until the final all-clear was sounded.

One night my father arrived home looking very tired and frightened. He said they had been sent to Coventry when the Germans struck there and on the way Luftwaffe fighters flying very low strafed them continuously. Those that got there safely had an enormous job dealing with an unprecedented amount of death and destruction in that city. Because of efforts to turn over-weight civilians into fit fireman, Dad didn't like the senior officer who relentlessly drilled him and his colleagues but he had to admit at the end of the war in 1945 he was fitter than he had ever been in his life.

There was one other incident at St Saviour's school when lessons were abruptly halted after an unexploded bomb was found not far away from the school premises. While the bomb disposal lads went to work we went back to our familiar places of safety. At least great grandfather enjoyed the occasion even though his apple stock was depleted once again.

As I approached the end of my time at primary school, I was allowed into the city to join up with friends or to visit my grandparents in Chapel Row. Amazingly they were still running the motor accessories shop despite their advancing years. It was only then that I realised the extent of the hammering Bath had taken from the Germans. Holes were torn in the Paragon where our good doctor had lived--- I just stood and looked at that for minutes in total horror---the Assembly Rooms used for lots of civic and social functions were just a shell and even the hospitals I had visited over the years for odd bits of treatment were badly damaged. But most shocking was the state of hundreds of homes, totally wrecked or not there any more; like Dorothy's house in the Wizard of Oz, whisked away on an evil east wind.

Young as I was, I couldn't stop myself standing by the remains of houses that had once stood tall and proud and wondered how many Bath people died there or had perhaps escaped earlier just as my family had done.

4

At Last—Something to Celebrate

Some memories may have dimmed with the passing years but there was no forgetting the joy of the VE Day celebrations. We had travelled in our old Morris 8 to my aunt and uncle's house in Golders Green, a part of London which had not been a serious German target. Aunt Wynne and Uncle Bus were not relatives but friends of the family but we loved them to bits and not just because they were the proud owners of one of the first black and white television sets. Watching early children's programmes from Alexandra Palace was really something to talk about when we got back to school. But there was something about Golders Green and London generally which gave me a big thrill and I didn't mind the painfully slow car journey from Bath to the big city. We all joined the large crowds outside Buckingham Palace on VE Day and cheered wildly when the King and Queen stepped onto the balcony accompanied by the two princesses and Prime Minister, Winston Churchill. In a huge crowd the only way I could see what was going on was from my father's shoulders. It's a wonderful memory but at the time rather frightening for a chap still short of a few inches and easily knocked about by the excited crowd.

More enjoyable was our first holiday after the war years, a long drive to Morecambe where the recollections are not so much of the sea, more of the extraordinary breakfasts, buttered toast a rasher of bacon and **two** eggs. We were soon to get our first banana and a small increase in our miserly sweets ration. On a later trip into Minehead I was introduced to a knickerbocker glory, a towering mixture of fruit and ice-cream served in a vessel something like a champagne glass but three times higher. It made a big impression; 70 years later my eyes still glisten when I see that treat on a restaurant menu. At the right moment and in a secluded place I might give it another try.

The celebrations had to end sometime and when they did they signalled a change in our lives. As soon as the fire brigade let him go, Dad set his heart on joining old colleagues in a project to create a newspaper in Bristol which would compete with Harmsworth's Evening World, a brash tabloid more concerned with giving away sets of china as bribes, than producing a truly local newspaper. With a couple of old typewriters and a range of orange boxes as chairs, a small group of men had already set about the task of producing *'the newspaper all Bristol asked for and helped to create.'* That message formed part of the newspaper's logo until very recently.

But Dad had a competing interest, or perhaps it would be more accurate to describe it as a competing problem. The grandparents were getting too old to run the motor accessories shop in Chapel Row and my crazy parents decided to take on the challenge themselves. The war was over so there was no danger of another conflagration but neither Ann nor I were keen on leaving Brunswick Street to live in the centre of the city. Bath's Georgian houses are prized possessions today but we saw them as rambling, even ugly buildings made more depressing by the dirty coloured Bath stone. What we didn't realise when the move was made was that our father would spend most of his life in Bristol and our mother, as well as looking after us, would have to run the shop.

No one considered the impact the addition of a complicated business would have on the lives of the younger members of the family. Motor accessory shops don't exist today but were vital in the 50s and 60s when small local garages relied on a supply of parts to keep none too reliable cars of that period on the road. When I say complicated I mean complicated. Although this shop was hardly larger than an ice-cream parlour it was festooned with an almost unbelievable variety of parts. Fan-belts, for example, hung in rows and a special catalogue had to be on hand to ascertain which belt belonged to which car. Then there were gaskets, hosepipes, drawers of multi-shaped washers, as well as headlight and sidelight bulbs. In a shed, in what passed as a garden were cans of anti-freeze, the flammable contents putting us all in far more danger than any of Hitler's bombs. Health and safety regulations were not quite what they are today. Oh, I should not forget the snow chains of various shapes and sizes that Ann and I would trip over as we tried to negotiate a way to the front door to go to school.

There was another little quirk to this business....nobody ever paid for anything on the spot. Garage mechanics were always in a hurry to satisfy impatient motorists so an invoice had to be made out for every transaction. When Dad got back from his Bristol job, usually very late, he disappeared into a pokey little office with Mum where together they made out invoices, checked stock and re-ordered whatever was necessary. They were lucky if they finished in time for a quick visit to the renovated Francis Hotel for a much needed nightcap.

My grandfather had grandly named his shop West of England Motor Industries which became shortened to WOEMI. My mother became known as Mrs Woemi (pronounced wee-me) and the efficiency with which she ran the shop did become well-known all over the West Country. Ann and I also became involved, frequently answering the door at unsocial hours to meet the request of a garage proprietor 'desperately keen' to help a stranded motorist. As we also took part in the annual stocktaking, a horrendous task counting every little washer, belt and plug in the shop, we also became quite handy at finding the right gasket or piece of hose to satisfy an impatient customer. At least it gave Mum a break.

Because our parents worked so hard, Ann and I had to fend for ourselves, looking for activities which would give us a break from life over the shop. Ann was an enthusiastic member of the girl guides and I divided my attention between practising in the nets at Bath Cricket Club and singing with the choir at St Michael's Church. When I reflect on this latter activity today it grieves me that my approach to church life was so casual and to a large extent meaningless. Choir boys lived in a bubble, rehearsing when told to but rarely doing anything which furthered their understanding of Christianity. The services were considered to be boring events and I have no memory of the vicar ever taking us to one side to explain the part Jesus Christ played in our lives. St Michaels was at the end of the street where we lived and this certainly had its disadvantages. Until I joined the choir it didn't much matter but having been promoted to 'top boy' living within a few yards of the vestry door made me very vulnerable to scorn and official disapproval. When father decided on a Sunday he should stop working and take the family off to the seaside, I had to creep into the car knowing that the choirmaster, Mr Pickwick, was standing in the entrance to the church vestry showing displeasure and making it quite clear what he thought about one of his choir boys going off to play on the sands of Weston super Mare when there were anthems to be sung.

I gained little from the traditional morning and evening services and it was fairly common practice for choir boys to seek inappropriate diversions. This was more difficult after my 'promotion' which meant I was up front, very visible and from time to time called upon to sing a solo. When this happened Mum and Dad came to listen but they never discussed the sermon or made any mention of other aspects of the service and so with sadness I still query whether they had a meaningful faith. The same could be said of the choirmaster and the vicar who carried out their basic functions conscientiously but without creating any particular relationships with the people around them, particularly with younger members of the congregation. But from this distance in space and time should I be making these conjectures? I suspect not; later in life I discovered my mother regularly prayed in the privacy of her bedroom. And one of her prayers would almost certainly have been about the tragic death of her father when she was only ten years-of-age. Later when the time came to turn out her treasure chest of mementoes, I discovered an array of photographs and cards sent to his wife and children at Christmas time. Each is a collector's item in its own right but one particular card demonstrates the heartache of losing a loved one just as the Armistice was being signed. It reads:

> *In loving memory of my dear husband*
>
> Sapper Elisha (Bert) Gould
> *Royal Engineers*
> Who fell in battle in France, 3rd September 1918
>
> *After accomplishing an important bridging operation on which the success of the battle depended.*
>
> Aged 40 years
> *He died that we might live*

On a later caravan holiday we drove the length and breath of Northern France to trace my grandfather's grave in the Merville Communal Cemetery. The photograph we took of my mother standing at the side of the grave has pride of place in what I call my Generation Book. It is a photograph which I hope will be treasured by generations to come as a reminder of the sacrifices made to secure their future.

There was nothing noteworthy about my school days or those of my sister. Ann went to the City of Bath Girls' School and I trudged to the top of Beecham Cliff to the boys' section with an equally unimaginative title. Both were grammar schools and I have to be honest and say that under the conditions existing then, we both struggled. We were not dim but we weren't very academic either. Examinations for me were a nightmare and the struggle to survive still haunts my dreams.

We both walked to and from school on a regular basis. And that meant tackling a hill after a cross city trek. My last stretch was locally named Jacob's ladder, a series of steps up the perilous slopes of Beecham Cliff. It was either that route or the long way round, not a good choice on the day the curriculum said we had to tackle a three and a half mile cross-country course.

The City of Bath Boys' School produced its occasional sporting celebrity, the most notable being Roger Bannister, the first four-minute miler. But it was not a school which cared for all its pupils and with hindsight one wishes the comprehensive system had been given more of a chance. For the talented, maybe the top 30 per cent of students who were in line for a university place, the grammar school was a fine environment, but in my school and in so many similar establishments the other 70 per cent were left to fend for themselves. My very snooty headmaster had no career advice for me apart from predicting that I would probably finish up selling newspapers like my father. The 'slight' was intentional because he knew my father held a responsible position on a regional newspaper but chose to imply we were newspaper 'sellers' promoting our wares in newsagents' shops and on street corners.

The headmaster was right about one thing. I was heading for a career in newspapers but on a very different level to the one he had mapped out for me. My father, now in the middle of a fight between the powerful Harmsworth paper, the Evening World, and the fledging Bristol Evening Post, pulled strings to get me taken on as a cub reporter, a job for which I was entirely unsuited. Neither of us took into account that my writing skills and my temperament were quite foreign to a job of this nature and I would suffer long months of terror and mental torture. I have always excused myself by claiming I was 'a slow starter' and needed more time to develop. True this may have been but it was madness to enter a job for which I had had no training. And I was not alone. Many young people who didn't go to university or college will recall that they 'stumbled' into a job, probably one that happened to be advertised on the jobs-vacant page as they were leaving the classroom for the last time.

Blame my school I may do, but I have to take some of the stick for making such a catastrophic start to my life's career. When important examinations were looming I was far more interested in tracking the occupants of the City of Bath Girls School. Rumour has it that I was seen to drop a glove in the path of one young lady in a blatant attempt to catch her attention but my behaviour didn't quite compare with the licentious behaviour of previous well-known Bath residents. I was no Beau Nash but none the less earned a reputation which got in the way of anything like serious study. I also spent hours in the nets at Bath Cricket Club, another activity leaving me short on time for necessary bookwork.

5

Struggles of a Cub Reporter

Because of my lack of academic achievement, I made life very hard for myself on moving into the Evening Post newsroom. Twice a week it was night school; essential law for journalists, central and local government, use of language and the worst abomination of all ... shorthand and typing. In addition, the news editor, a man I eventually came to admire, would send me out on two, even three, evening assignments that often left me stranded in different parts of Bristol without any transport. I will never know how I handled the rambling words of the Rotary Club guest speaker while still trying to cope with lesson four of the Pitman's shorthand course.

Back in the office my tactic was to conceal myself behind a desk at the back of the newsroom in the hope that everyone would forget all about me. They didn't...not for very long. A regular duty was charting ships in and out of Avonmouth docks (this was in case a vessel got into trouble on the other side of the world and the sub-editor could then write in a line that the ship called at Avonmouth on such and such a date).

Other jobs for junior reporters were writing up weddings from submitted details, standing at church doors recording the names of funeral congregations and logging the results of rabbit, bird and dog shows. Among the hazards were mixing up the wedding forms and marrying a couple a week too early; not including the name of a mourner who had slipped into a funeral ten minutes late; and failing to print the correct initials of the winner of the best-dog-in-show trophy.

The truth of the matter was, I should never have been given the job; my spelling was atrocious and my use of language was such that it was necessary to take another examination to lift my literary skills to somewhere near the standard required today for a decent 'A'level equivalent. But I survived mainly by displaying an almost fanatical enthusiasm, jumping off buses to file stories about car crashes I came across on my regular journeys between home (Bath) and work (Bristol). I was happier telephoning a story than having to slowly and painfully hammer the keys of a typewriter. Being out of the office also meant I could escape the wrath of sub-editors who would delight in turning my copy into confetti and suggesting I might be better considering a career as a window cleaner.

A common complaint against reporters, especially young and inexperienced ones, is they exaggerate to make their piece more exciting. It was only a matter of time before I fell into that trap. Sent to describe traffic conditions during a particularly heavy snow storm, I was the perpetrator of a headline which described 8ft snow drifts from which cars had to be hauled. Even four feet would have been an exaggeration. The Automobile Association was not amused when they were inundated with calls for alternatives routes. Nor was my news editor when the AA complained about the disruption caused.

My tendency not to take my studies as seriously as I should continued and having joined up with John Stevens, who was to become the respected rugby correspondent of the Bath Chronicle, we would escape to the Bristol News Theatre if we didn't fancy another evening studying the idiosyncrasies of local government. Somehow we managed to get away with our waywardness. What I was not getting away with was my poor performance as a reporter. The hand-to-hand battle between the wealthy Evening World and the struggling-to-survive Evening Post meant that the two editorial teams were constantly going head-to-head to score points over each other. If the reporter's afternoon commission was an inquest opening at 3.0pm, a messenger boy was sent to grab the first 100 words scribbled on a grubby piece of copy paper. This was whisked back to HQ so that the opening of the inquest could be recorded in the last edition of the day.

Few readers could ever have been aware of the lengths their local papers went to beat each other to the draw but the competition certainly kept the editorial reporting teams on their toes. It kept me in a permanent state of panic which did nothing to improve my performance. One way of putting me out of sight and out of mind was to lose me for a day in the Divorce Court where it was thought I could do little harm. Scattered through the scrap book which I kept from day one (goodness knows why because I had little to be proud of) are a number of items with the same deadly heading **Decrees Nisi.**

The rule was that in undefended cases, where one of the partners admitted being the cause of the breakdown, all that could be reported were the names of the couple and the grounds on which the divorce was granted---desertion, adultery, misconduct or cruelty. No one could have had any regard for what my future attitude to marriage might be because of the endless number of times I was forced to spend listening to details of how private detectives had noticed strange goings-on at odd times of the night. For the first time I realised that husbands, too, could suffer abuse from a wife who had mastered the art of using kitchen implements as weapons.

During the post-lunch session there was a tendency for observers to find their eyes becoming heavy and this nearly led to my downfall. Opening one eye I noticed the senior reporter from the opposition paper was doing some furious note-taking. The judge was droning on and I would have been in serious trouble if Cyril Ling hadn't taken pity on me and reminded me that in defended cases the judgement could be reported. Opposition scribe he may have been but he earned my undying friendship by offering a helping hand in catching up with the judge's condemnation of one of the wayward partners. If Cyril had wanted to wreck my fledgling career he could have fed me with alarming rubbish which would have put me back in court to answer a contempt charge.

My scrap book was a constant source of amusement to the more experienced editorial staff but it gave me something to do if the news editor couldn't find an assignment suited to my lowly ability. Thumbing through it years later, it does throw an interesting light on the totally different way a local newspaper recorded the happenings of the community it served.

In 1953 the Coronation of Queen Elizabeth was about to happen and when I was not listening to divorce cases, I became the street party correspondent. Some 250 streets in Bristol were planning traffic-disrupting celebrations and nobody seemed to mind. Each street was allocated a small space in the Post in which it could tell other citizens what they were going to do, down to the details of the sandwiches they were planning to make and the types of cakes that would be baked in scores of ovens. Ignoring my failure to grasp basic maths, I assessed that thousands of yards of flag materials would be sewn together and I even asked music shops whether they were getting a run on any particular type of instrument. To my amazement, one shop said it could sell a big drum and a pair of cymbals every day. They were needed for the many planned processions. Recorders and mouth organs were also gaining in popularity. It wasn't exactly a scoop but I was able to score one over the opposition by revealing that silver spoons would be given to all babies born in Southmead Hospital on Coronation Day. No experienced journalist was going to be asked to plod the streets of Bristol on the big day, so the privilege came to me and whereas those celebrating seemed to dodge the wind and the rain, I finished up looking like a drowned rat. Ignoring the water which was dripping down the back of my neck, I reported that 'the bad weather had not dampened the spirits of party organisers or those who were determined to make the day special.' With my expertise on Coronation matters established, I was given the task of tracking down those who had been successful in the draw for a seat on the Coronation route. For some, success in winning a seat was every bit as thrilling as being awarded tickets for the Olympic Games in 2012.

Something had to fill the vacuum after all this excitement and I sensed what was coming my way; the Women's Institutes, a weekly column recording the names of ladies who had excelled themselves in the decorated egg cup competition or produced the most imaginative papier-mâché table decoration. With great solemnity, I also reported that several institutes had stood for three minutes in silent tribute to Queen Mary, who had recently died.

Rabbit shows were very popular in the smaller communities around Bristol and I was probably the first journalist to report that a Netherland Dwarf, the size of a small rat, had won a record four classes. As scoops go that must have rated in the top ten. If it wasn't rabbits then the office diary nearly always featured an above average number of pending dog and bird shows. It was death to the reporter who managed to mix up his unflighted yellow cocks with his light green hens. News Editors could get quite touchy if their phones were blocked for hours with complaints from angry 'fanciers.'

It was a great relief to see on the daily diary that at last I was to get a couple of assignments with the prospects of a decent headline. I was to interview the parents of Pte Frank Perryman who had been captured in Korea. They had received a Christmas card and a letter which indicated he was in good health and would be home much sooner than expected.

Then during a 'flu epidemic, when the newsroom was almost empty, I was let off the leash to cover the launching of a new ship at Avonmouth Docks. I knew these events were a challenge because I had seen the sorry state of senior colleagues when returning from this arduous duty. They had arrived back at the office on legs refusing to follow the directions being transmitted by the brain. As tradition decreed, champagne had certainly bubbled down the side of the shiny new merchant ship but far more had touched bottom in the bellies of all those gathered to witness the occasion. Still in my teens, it was probably not surprising that my self-control was sub zero. When I called to file my story---an hour too late for the afternoon edition---my surprisingly tolerant news editor listened to my ramblings and sweetly commented: 'You're quite sure it was not you they launched today.' He thought it advisable to save my wobbly attempts at constructing a story for the next day's edition.

There was no let up in the disdain and ridicule expressed by sub-editors almost on a daily basis. Most of them knew I was occupying a reporter's desk because my father was one of the newspaper's executives and they resented that. But even if my writing was well below par, I was gradually developing a news sense that was going to serve me well in the years ahead. Reporting a railway horse and harness competition may sound mundane today, but I was able to dig out the fact that because of the decreasing number of these magnificent animals, it was likely to be the last competition of its kind.

The quality of my story writing continued to improve and this was illustrated when I interviewed the husband of a shorthand typist who was attending four-power talks in East Berlin. She had written to her husband, casually mentioning she had gone shopping without an escort.. You just didn't do that sort of thing on the other side of the Berlin wall and her husband was horrified. She came home still wondering what all the fuss was about.

6

Celebrities Galore

It is fascinating to pick out some of the international names who found themselves in the news when they stepped out into the regions, people like singer Guy Mitchell, pianist Semprini, comedian Alfred Marks, boxer Randolph Turpin, England Gloucestershire cricketer W.R. Hammond; also actors such as Jack Warner, Claude Hulbert, Mai Zetterling, Sonnie Hale and Dennis Price, to mention just a few. Johnny Ray performed in Bristol's Colston Hall and 160 youngsters camped out all night to make sure of a ticket. During the one time in his life when he lost some of his shine, Frank Sinatra made a solo appearance at the Bristol Hippodrome. But he was amazing, wandering onto the stage with a cup of tea and eventually getting around to a song after a very informal chat with the audience. He looked a very tiny and lonely figure on that huge stage but had everyone in raptures.

I was still out of my depth in many respects but treasured the headline over my story about a small dog- -- *Police Pursue Petrified Prize Poodle,* featuring *Rothara the Smuggler of Panavon (Smuggie* for short*)* with 80 first prizes to its name. It leapt to freedom from its owner's car in Castle Street and defied everyone as it dodged moving traffic. All seemed to be lost but when the owner reached her office she found her very valuable canine sitting outside her office wagging its tale. There was a short excursion into the political world when Anthony Wedgwood Benn was making his first attempt to become the Labour candidate for Bristol south-east. My shorthand was just good enough to record a typical Benn onslaught *'the Conservative Party appeals to the worst instincts of the people…it's everyone for themselves under that regime.'*

If I had been able to see into the future my assignment to listen to the General Secretary of the Lord's Day Observance Society might have had greater significance. But it was the job no other reporter wanted to do and to be truthful my life-style in my teens certainly didn't demonstrate any respect for Sunday as a day of rest. Often I worked harder on the seventh day than on most other days of the week and I felt little sympathy for the society's general secretary when he used the occasion to complain about the lack of a coherent message among the churches. He exclaimed passionately: 'All is lost if we bicker over what should and what should not be done on the Sabbath.' Those words were to revisit me with considerable force but not for many more years.

A prized possession for a young would-be journalist was a by-line and my first was drooled over unashamedly, the uncovering of a dwelling from the Mesolithic period (between the Ice Age and the New Stone Age). Archaeologists were overcome with excitement and fortunately one of them virtually wrote the article for me. Even my arch enemy, the sub-editor with a faint likeness to Hitler, acknowledged that for once he didn't have to undertake a massive re-writing exercise.

My overall rocky performance convinced me that even the near presence of my father would not save me from the boot. But when all seemed to be lost one editorial executive, possibly possessed with the desire to see the back of me, put forward a swim-or-sink suggestion designed to strike fear into the heart of a much stronger character than me. I suspected that the sub-editor who mocked my attempts to extract stories from dog shows in Shirehampton and church fetes in Fishponds, may have had something to do with the decision.

What was about to happen was an amazing period of my life which would eventually turn me into a journalist with some fire in his belly. After a surprise interview with the editor, I was told that I was going to be 'put in charge' of the Bath office. 'Put in charge'…whatever did that mean? I was still several weeks short of my nineteenth birthday and even in my own estimation (especially in my own estimation) quite incapable of taking over the reins of a branch office of a fast-growing regional evening newspaper.

An understanding of the relationship between two great but very different West Country cities has to be taken into account before any sense can be made of the task I was about to undertake. Putting it very mildly, the citizens of both cities didn't like each other. The difference between a Bathonian and a Bristolian was on a par with the difference between a Yorkshire man and a Lancastrian. Despite this brittle relationship the Evening Post decided it would try to persuade the Bath population it would get a far better news service from a much more experienced set-up, albeit with its headquarters a further 12 miles down the A4. The plan was to bring out an early edition with all the news the local Bath Chronicle editorial team would struggle to catch up with later in the day. My brief was to arise at the crack of dawn, grab any piece of news I could snatch from the police, fire and ambulance services and send 'dramatic' copy in time for an early edition. The bill posters might read 'Three dead in Bath road pile-up' and the Post would sell hundreds of copies before the Chronicle reporters were out of bed. In theory, it sounded like a stimulating brief. With the prospect of abandoning my daily journey to Bristol and not having to suffer regular failure to catch the last bus home in the evening (the night watchman at the Silver Street offices of the Post never quite came to terms with finding me sleeping on a camp bed in the newsroom) the future looked rosier.

I approached my new office in the Lower Borough Walls in Bath with a lightness of step which indicated a touch of expectation, even a tinge of excitement. Such emotions were not going to survive even the first five steps into the little dungeon about to become my new workplace. Quite what it had been used for was difficult to fathom but it certainly gave the impression that little attempt had been made to make it habitable since a bomb in near-by Southgate Street had blown the stuffing out of it some 13 years previously. It consisted of two rooms, one almost filled by the contraption that fudged the latest racing results into the stop press, the other containing one ancient desk and a rickety chair presumably thought good enough for the newly appointed Bath office chief reporter. Until this time the job had been done by Dick Ledbury, a freelance with a strong resemblance to Beau Nash and a tendency to conduct himself in like manner. On the wall next to the desk was a telephone, of the type most people will have seen in museums or on the set of old movies. It had one huge advantage; the line was never busy because it was a direct link with Bristol activated by twirling a handle. This rapid circular movement caused a bell to ring 12 miles away and with luck someone would be around to transfer your best story of the day onto small pieces of scruffy paper. The established practice was for a girl with headphones and a typewriter to type not more than two paragraphs per sheet. In theory this would enable the early part of a story to be on its way to the typesetter before the reporter had wound up his account.

Again the motivation was speed, to be seen to be a faster operator than the opposition. Television and other modern means of communication put paid to this quaint means of giving the public instant access to printed news, both local and national. In the 21st century if the Town Hall goes up in flames, its demise is recorded on television before the embers have cooled and long before the local newspaper can land on the doormats of its readers.

I soon learned that one of the most irritating distractions (despite the attempts at discipline by the office manager, Charlie Maggs) was the comings and goings of the newspaper sellers, nearly always in various states of inebriation. One of them was so aggressive in his selling methods that few Bathonians had the nerve to walk away from him. He did his bit for sales but not much to enhance the relationship between Bath and Bristol.

Within weeks our feeble little operation was transferred to another part of the city, not in the interests of improved conditions for staff but to overcome some dispute about rental charges. The new office in Kingsmead Square (yards from another huge bombsite) was a former cake shop still sporting its original bizarre wallpaper and equipped with the shelves once used to display cake and biscuit products. An impressive new development was the installation of a teleprinter, a very disconcerting means of communication because once the reporter had committed himself to a bundle of facts there was no going back. The words appeared simultaneously in Bristol and any change of mind or realisation that you had said an important local businessman had pleaded guilty to drink driving when in fact his plea was 'not guilty' had to be put right by frantic corrections. There was no guarantee that the teleprinter operator would not have left for his beer break when the revised version arrived.

But I am getting ahead of myself. I would be doing the reader and myself a disservice if I did not share the horror of my first days as a branch office reporter. My new job with its description, chief reporter (Bath Office), may have sounded impressive but it was obvious no one in head office had given any serious thought as to what the job might entail. I can only imagine they were thinking in terms of letting me loose in a large village where little happened beyond the usual mundane activities of a much smaller and inferior community.

But Bath was a city! The only difference between Bath and Bristol was that Bath had a smaller population and was more compact (a blessing because in the early days the only transport I had was a bicycle). Daily events in Bristol were covered by as many as 18 to 20 reporters, several of them devoting their time to specialities like crime, local government, the courts, cinema, the theatre, motoring, the arts, business and, of course, sport, with further divisions for coverage of soccer, rugby, cricket, athletics and speedway. There was no understanding of the fact that the City of Bath could parallel all these activities apart from speedway. To make up for this deficiency the city staged the biggest dog show in the country and was famous for its annual music festival.

John Alexander was expected to take care of the lot and received help only on those occasions when the story was important enough to tempt a mature Bristol journalist into grabbing some of the glory for himself. This was certainly the case with the notorious John Straffen child murders, frequently on the front pages of most national newspapers. Straffen, who had lived with his family in Bath and had killed two young girls in the summer of 1951, was found unfit to plea and was committed to Broadmoor Hospital. He escaped and murdered another child. It had been the Bath Medical Officer of Health who had ruled he was insane and as far as journalists were concerned whenever this ugly story reared its head it was always to Bath they headed. I moved to the Bath office as this story was in the process of being wound up so I escaped the possibility of baptism by fire, a great relief bearing in mind all the other hurdles in front of me.

7

Tackling the Impossible

Realistically, a 19-year-old reporter working in a city with a recognised and much loved local newspaper of its own was not going to have an easy time. Apart from meeting more experienced newsmen on just about every self chosen assignment, some city officials found it difficult to take me seriously and were not slow in making me aware of the fact. There was also a matter of trust. Would they think me capable of handling important information intended to keep the public on their side and be able to present it in a manner they thought appropriate? And would they be able to stomach the idea that an outsider, not long out of senior school and from that 'distasteful' city of Bristol, would be constantly examining their affairs and asking awkward questions. An early task was to try to make friends with the Chief Constable, a Detective Superintendent, a Mayor, a Town Clerk, the City Coroner, heads of both fire and ambulance brigades, not to mention managers of football, rugby clubs, theatres and the secretaries of various businessmen's clubs.

A big question that no one seemed to have considered was how I would manage to attend a council meeting, a magistrate's court, an inquest, a local government inquiry and cover all that was happening from Batheaston to Twerton at the same time. The strain started from week one with a full meeting of Bath City Council. So that businessmen could attend, the meeting started at 5.0pm and went on for six or seven hours.

That meant absorbing a lot of politically tainted debate, initially about subjects that were completely foreign to me. On the press bench were usually three Chronicle reporters, sometimes four, who worked in relays. As each completed their allotted time they scurried back to their office to write up their accounts before heading home for supper.

Red-eyed and with a notebook stuffed with shorthand, much of it unreadable, I returned to my 'cakeshop' after midnight with the task of unravelling huge amounts of material before slowly, very slowly, transferring the product of my efforts to Bristol via the teleprinter. Eventually, the brain rebelled and I had to give up trying to make sense of inarticulate outbursts by pompous councillors who loved to hear their own voice. I suspected that the paragraph or two that did appear in an unwanted rival newspaper attracted a very small readership!

One man who sympathised with the uneven battle I was trying to fight was Bath's colourful Chief Constable, George Nichols. He loved publicity and this worked in my favour. When the local or national newshounds gave him a bad time he would get his own back, either by giving me an early tip-off or holding back a scrap or two of information I could use exclusively. He was one of the first to detect that despite my youth and inexperience I had an acute news sense and because of this an interesting relationship started to develop between us.

The first big story to break was one I would have had little chance of putting together effectively and legally if George Nichols had not given me a helping hand. No tip-off ever came direct from the top but it was not long before I realised I was cultivating one or two good friends. The story was a shocker even by today's standards. A man had walked up to the window of a GP's surgery, pushed a shot-gun through the glass and shot him dead.

I knew that if I informed Bristol too early, crime reporter Joe Gallagher, would be on the scene, brushing me aside with the claim that such a serious crime could not be left to a junior reporter. So I headed for the surgery and gathered enough information to give the Bristol sub-editors the surprise of their life when a presentable story started to filter through the teleprinter. A man, later revealed to be the husband of a woman who believed his wife was having an affair with the doctor, was quickly charged and that meant my report had to be restricted to the bare details. In today's lax climate, the man would have been instantly named and tried by the media no doubt with graphic pictures on the front page. The contempt of court restriction which has been largely ignored for most of the last decade was not one to be messed about with at that time. Today anything goes.

Unlike many journalists, I really enjoyed court work even a complicated fraud case. One downside was being a heavy smoker. I found long sessions a great strain and had to find moments to escape for a quick drag. On the plus side, after a month or two I started to forge some good relationships with two or three of the Chronicle reporters. Although we would never share any story considered an exclusive, there was always an understanding that if it was necessary to leave a court, committee or council chamber for any reason, someone else in the press box would fill in the gaps. This worked to everyone's advantage.

Court work did have its colourful and amusing moments. A case that had us all rushing about featured an elderly couple who appeared to have had a serious quarrel with dire consequences. The prosecution case was that matters got out of hand and the husband had struck his wife on the head with an axe. The press box was full when the man appeared accused of attempted murder. Reporters shared looks of astonishment as the wife appeared, head bandaged, but looking quite well in the circumstances. She gave her husband a beautiful smile and a wave as she took her seat. The prosecution said the husband admitted striking his wife but insisted he had not done this in anger. 'But what were you doing with an axe?' the prosecuting solicitor asked. The magistrate called the husband forward and said he wanted to hear an explanation from his own lips. It was the only time I have witnessed a crowd of cynical reporters break into spontaneous laughter during the hearing of a charge as serious as attempted murder. The husband said they were reciting nursery rhymes, acting them out at the same time. When they came to the line *'Here comes a candle to light you to bed...and here comes a chopper to chop off your head',* he swung the axe he was holding and accidentally struck her skull. Trying not to smile the magistrate warned them both it was dangerous to mess about with dangerous weapons and gave the husband a conditional discharge. They walked out of the court hand-in-hand.

There were many farcical aspects to this 'mission impossible' handed to me at such a tender age. One of them was the necessity to write 'running' reports on the Saturday matches of Bath City, a non-league soccer club, hobbling along with the help of ageing players like Stan Mortensen and Charlie Fleming. My first match was quite an experience for the simple reason that I had never watched an entire soccer match in my life. I was a rugby fan and would have been delighted to spend my Saturday afternoons on the Recreation Ground where Bath had built up a fine reputation as one of the country's top teams. But for years a freelance with an established reputation had covered the fortunes of Bath rugby and I was not given a look-in. Instead, I had to take a quick course in the rules of soccer and try to pick up the jargon of the game as I went along.

A lot of my time was spent in Bath's Guildhall, which housed the offices and meeting chamber of Bath City Council, the Mayor's Parlour, the Magistrates' Courts and a banqueting room where all the important civic functions were held. The king-pin in the Guildhall was the Town Clerk, Jared E. Dixon, who ruled his staff with a rod of iron. The full council met at regular intervals but various committees---housing, planning, health, surveying etc--- met during the intervening time. One committee clerk had the huge task of keeping track of all these meetings but he did have secretaries and typists to take minutes and perform other tasks to keep the committee members informed.

For all sorts of reasons tape recorders were not favoured in those days, so a good shorthand writer was a valuable asset and one of these valuable assets was a teenage girl called Susan. Her social life overlapped with mine so it was not long before we were meeting at dances and other events for young adults. An unlikely relationship started to develop, unlikely because we were convinced the Town Clerk would not take kindly to one of his secretaries being friendly with a newspaper reporter, even if he did work for that 'foreign' Bristol newspaper. If we were going to continue meeting we had to convince this formidable man that we could be trusted. I promised him that I would make no attempt to extract information from Susan and the fact that we managed to keep this up meant I was able to form a working relationship with Jared and several members of his staff. This was tested when the nationals got hold of a story about a young girl, Mary Ford, being taken away from her foster parents without any apparent reason. The committee making decisions in this case came under fire and I had to take special care not to let my enthusiasm to get hold of an exclusive tempt me into using a piece of information that could well be classed as a leak. My teenage relationship with Susan did have one sticky patch but that was more to do with a young man's desire to play the field than a quarrel with city officials.

Bath was beginning to recover from the pasting it took during the war years but only very slowly. The National Trust wanted to re-build the blitzed Assembly Rooms but many thought the initial contract of £60,000 was a waste of money with so many other derelict sites in the city demanding attention. Few could think of any uses for the rooms and claimed that a purpose-built concert hall would be a much better alterative to what would surely become a White Elephant. Another priority in many people's minds was the cleaning up of the Bath stone on many of its historic buildings. On a visit to the city for the first time, one small boy was heard to comment: 'Daddy, when did they have a fire here?' Fires there may have been during the blitz but the intense bombing could not be blamed for the state of the Bath stone which was certainly pristine when it was mined but had discoloured badly over the years. Bath Abbey was first on the list for a specialised clean-up and it worked so well that one American asked a rather different question: 'When did they decide to rebuild the Abbey?' His question was answered when he walked to the rear of the building and saw just how grubby it still was from a different angle.

Another piece of refurbishment was to a hostelry next to the Theatre Royal, known as the Garricks Head. It was bought by Beau Nash in 1720 and he turned a room on the first floor into a gambling den. The building was given its name because it housed a bust of the actor, David Garrick, apparently obtained by Beau Nash from a sculptor in lieu of a gambling debt. The building was reputed to have a ghost that drifted next door to the Theatre Royal when it got bored. A regular visitor in slightly more modern times was the English playwright, Tom Stoppard, who worked on a morning newspaper in Bristol and suffered with me and other young West Country hopefuls on the first official training course for young journalists. He was a natural critic and the Theatre Royal, together with the Old Vic in Bristol, was his training ground. The Garricks Head provided the much needed after show refreshment and was a convenient base for scribbling reviews of shows that had to be filed for the following day's paper

What a different attitude we had to our Royal Family in the 50s! Columns of newsprint were given over to a pending visit of the Queen and Duke of Edinburgh to the Georgian city. But this was no special occasion; the Royal party was simply 'calling in' on their way to Badminton for a private visit. Even so, elaborate plans were made for the half hour stop-over in Bath. Extensive route plans were drawn up as well as defined gathering points to get a brief glimpse of proceedings before the Queen and Duke entered the Guildhall. Pensioners, hospital patients and school children were given a high priority. Those inside the Guildhall complained they had less chance of seeing the Queen than those on the pavement outside.

***

Should we have come to the conclusion that the behaviour of today's young people is so much worse than in the 50s and 60s, we would do well to examine the cult of the 'Teddy Boys' who, apart from adopting a form of Edwardian dress, went around in packs looking for trouble. Police guards had to travel on trains between Bath and Bristol because of the regular fights that occurred. Contrary to stories that circulated at the time, they were not responsible for stealing a weather cock from the 230ft spire of a Bath church. Courage and daring were not two of the qualities they were known for. Sadly, the thief had second thoughts about cashing in on his achievement because the weather cock was found at the bottom of the River Avon broken into small pieces.

8

To Paris without Love

Right in the middle of a period when I was enjoying being a newspaper reporter for the first time. I had to dig out my deferment papers (deferment was granted to those who were deemed to have important study to complete) and prepare for a period of national service. This was a particularly bitter pill to swallow because it was now 1956 and I was to be among the last young men to suffer this interference to their lives. Much to everyone's amazement I had proposed to Sue despite the prospect of being separated for most of the following two years. 'It won't last' was the comment I heard from more than one of my cynical friends. They predicted that I would receive a 'Dear John' letter within three months, probably something I deserved bearing in mind I had let her down badly on one occasion. Thankfully, our relationship was now much stronger and we were quite convinced we would be planning our wedding in 1959.

But first I had to suffer a period of training at Willems Barrack, Aldershot---blocks of troop accommodation built for the 1st Cavalry Brigade in 1856. This horror block of buildings was named Willems after a famous cavalry victory in 1794 during wars in the French revolution. There was one solid fuel heater in the centre of each barrack room which either smoked continuously or went out completely. The one loo was totally inadequate for 20-plus men and it blocked every few days, a situation which gave jumped-up regular regimental police corporals a wonderful chance to exert their authority every time a new National Service recruit stepped out of line. The favourite punishment?...to unblock the loos. After six weeks of training---a mockery in the Royal Army Service Corps because most RASC national servicemen became drivers or clerks and two hours learning how to use a 303 rifle was not going to make them into a soldier---the battle to get a good posting started in earnest. I thought it strange that there were so many young, would-be journalists in my company but the reason soon became clear. The Army had calculated that most of us would have had some training in clerical skills, especially shorthand and typing, and the need to put us through exhaustive classroom routines was not necessary. My shorthand was far from perfect but it didn't seem to matter and I was presented with an impressive list of postings, some of them to quite exotic places. These did not interest me because my priority was to stay in England where I could make frequent visits home to see my fiancé.

My first choice, which after a successful interview seemed a certainty, was a clerical job in the Ministry of Defence. The Army had different ideas. Most young men would have been delighted but I was not a happy soldier when I was told I would be going to Supreme Headquarters Allied Powers Europe (SHAPE) which had quite splendid premises on the edge of Versailles, Paris. My protests fell on stony ground but my disappointment (considered unbelievable by many of my fellow trainee soldiers) was tempered by the news I was to become clerk to Field Marshall Viscount Montgomery, who in his dotage had been given the 'honorary' post of deputy to the Supreme Commander, General Lauris Norstad, an American. Even Susan understood that as much as she would have liked me to stay closer to home, it was the sort of experience I would remember for the rest of my life. So we smiled through our tears and started to make plans for her to visit Paris to celebrate her 21st birthday.

What no one told me was that by this time the Field Marshall had become a very temperamental old man and constantly blamed his national service clerks for the smallest matters that went wrong. And no one mentioned he could change his mind on a whim which was just what he did. This left me high and dry in what was called a holding company. A holding company was little better than hell on earth, ruled by a Company Quartermaster Sergeant, who took great delight in terrorising young men he considered too big for their boots. Just to suggest you had been to a grammar school was enough to send him into apoplexy. Once having taken a dislike to one of his charges he would trot out a whole series of objectionable punishments from cleaning out lavatories to painting blocks of stone protecting the grass in front of the officers' mess. Inevitably, he would consider neither job done to his satisfaction and would look for other ways to cause misery, like stopping a man's leave a few hours before he was due to leave camp or handing out the most hideous of cookhouse duties. As a rule, no one stayed in a holding company for more than a few days, 10 at the most, so when the summons for me to pack my bags and set off to Paris failed to materialise, I started to get very angry and dreadfully depressed. What I couldn't understand was that an order had been given to kit me out with the very best uniform, one that actually fitted, the reason being that I could not walk into the office of one of the British Army's most famous soldiers looking like a badly dressed tramp.

I may have thought of myself as being a bold reporter in the making but I was not much good at standing up for myself when a belligerent non-commissioned British Army officer decided I was easy meat for regular brow beating sessions. I look back on that time as the only occasion when I contemplated suicide. There was one short period of relief when I was sent off to do a special clerical job for an adjutant on Salisbury Plain. When I set out on a complicated train journey I must have created the impression that I was on my way to the 'front' of some imaginary war. Every piece of equipment had to go into a kit-bag and be carried on my not very sturdy shoulders. Having reached the nearest station to my destination, I must have looked a sorry sight trudging across a large section of Salisbury Plain, getting so tired that I considered dumping the kit-bag. Not a good idea if I wanted to avoid being put on a charge. The clerical work I was asked to do was not demanding and made a marvellous change from trying to unblock lavatories. Life was also made more amenable by working for an adjutant who was also a human being.

When the job was done I had to trudge back across the plain again weighed down by a kit-bag containing nothing of any use for the job I had been sent to do. A typical Army farce was awaiting me back at Willems Barracks. The guards on duty had no record of my impending return and on checking with the training company adjutant decided I had been posted. I was no longer expected and if I hadn't been such a coward I could have disappeared into thin air and never set foot in an army barrack room again. The temptation was great. But common sense prevailed as I knew they would catch up with me sooner or later and once back in civvy street I would not welcome a recall to face a desertion charge. So I reported back to CQMS Wolfe, who welcomed me with a leer that boded badly for the immediate future. I withstood the expected provocation for a while longer, then plucked up the courage to request a meeting with my commanding officer. To my surprise he actually apologised and explained that Montgomery had changed his mind and decided to hang on to his original clerk. To overcome my 'disappointment' he had arranged for me to be posted to SHAPE anyway to serve in another capacity. I think he was surprised at the look of despair that appeared on my face but how could I explain I had never wanted to go to Versailles in the first place?

An extra spell of leave made up for all those despairing moments when my holding company adversary had stopped me heading for the train at the last minute and I was able to regain some sanity by spending quality time with the girl I was going to marry. We made all sorts of plans and tried to make the time seem shorter by rigging up a calendar which allowed me to count off the days to demobilisation. The calendar stayed with me until the very last day of my service but by removing a single date each morning, it probably made the remaining 500-plus days seem even longer. I have to say that during those long separations, I became more attached to the white cliffs of Dover when they appeared on the horizon, than when they were disappearing into the distance. Our favourite song at the time was Nat King Cole crooning '*Back on the boat again, farewell to France*' but it was going to be a while before I could again appreciate those things I had always taken for granted, like home cooking and clean white sheets.

It would be untruthful to suggest that being trapped in a place like Paris was a thoroughly unpleasant experience. It was almost impossible for a young man not to enjoy one of the most beautiful cities in the world and not to wallow in some of its pleasures. A national serviceman's pay was derisory but that didn't stop us taking advantage of free bus rides (provided by the Americans) and heading for places like Longchamp for Sunday racing. It was a win or bust experience; either a spell of luck enabled us to ditch British Army cooking and dine in the American NAAFI or a complete wipe-out of the monthly pay packet meant a couple of weeks enduring foul smelling cabbage and chocolate steamed pudding. The consolation was to continue smoking ourselves to death as cigarettes were cheaper than a packet of peppermints. I had better not say what happened to the fast-growing cigarette mountain built up by the non smokers in case the Military Police are still active. They were not kind to any soldier, no matter what nationality, found sneaking down to the centre of Paris to make a dollar or two from surplus nicotine.

One of the perks of being on an American campus was the availability of buses which kept running until the early hours. Even if the last bus was missed it was not the most terrible experience to stay in the Latin Quarter all night listening to jazz, to sober up with onion soup in Pigalle and then catch the first transport back to camp at six in the morning. One all-night Parisian experience did go off the rails in an unexpected manner. Susan had plucked up courage to take a flight to Paris (she had never flown alone before) to celebrate her 21st birthday. I was like a cat on a hot tin roof all day much to the amusement of my fellow servicemen and it never occurred to me that working myself up into a pitch of excitement might spoil the enjoyment of the night ahead. We were to stay with a couple who were more permanently stationed at SHAPE, a naval writer and his wife who rented a small apartment in the suburbs. There was no transport to their home until the next day so we settled down to a romantic night on the streets of Paris. Sadly, it became anything but settled or romantic. All the anticipation had gone to my stomach and we had to make for the first (rather seedy) bar we could find so that I could have the security of the men's room, never the most salubrious of places in 20th century Paris.

Poor Susan was trapped at a table surrounded by heavily painted women who kept disappearing almost as frequently as her fiancé. They, of course, had other business in mind. Being a sweet little West Country girl with little experience of big city life, let alone Paris, it took her a while to work out that her company was a group of 'ladies of the night' meeting for their regular coffee break. Her innocence protected her from thinking she was being deserted by the man she loved seeking additional pleasures but she only had to look at his face, yellow and gaunt, to realise he was in no condition for anything other than a good dose of Imodium. During the night the condition of the patient improved and we were able to enjoy a morning coffee together in more congenial surroundings. The following short period of leave passed pleasantly enough but our days had a habit of starting so late that we never got to the Louvre and other attractions much before they were due to close! But we were happy enough walking by the Seine or observing the street artists in Montmartre.

Being one of 600 British soldiers at SHAPE was a fascinating experience. My daily workplace was the central registry where fellow workers included Americans, Dutch, Canadians and Belgians. It was a classic case of over-manning because all we had to do was to receive, log and distribute communications passing between all divisions of the North Atlantic Treaty Organisation. Some of the packages were marked secret or even Cosmic Top Secret but I was never allowed to inspect the contents. Having made a note of the elementary details such as time of arrival, date, classification and addressee, the package was carried by a messenger down one of the many corridors to be inspected by a senior officer from one of the 12 NATO countries represented. The job may have been boring but it was the British national servicemen who seemed to most appreciate the place where they had been posted. Some of the regulars, many at warrant officer level would boast that all they ever saw of Paris were the roads and buildings between the headquarters and the Gare du Nord. It didn't say much for British tastes that the delicious long crusty French loaves were rejected. Instead, 300 pounds of British-type loaves were made every night, confirming that the other ranks in the British Army were a pretty unimaginative lot.

One incident I would like to forget but never can was the outcome of playing a game called Jacks-up, inspired by the ridiculous low price of drinks in the international all-ranks canteen. As the cards went around the table it was agreed that the holder of the first jack named the drink (always a vicious combination that no cocktail barman would ever suggest), the second jack condemned the holder to pay for the drink, the third obliged the player to taste it and the fourth to drink it...all of it! It was a sad night when against the odds I finished up with the fourth jack on... I forget now just how many occasions. The outcome was disastrous. My timing was terrible because the next morning we were due for a CO's inspection and as the corporal in charge of my barrack room I was responsible for making sure it was spick and span. The guys who shared my quarters made sure the necessary work was done and told the inspecting party I was sick. It wasn't queried, which was just as well as they would have found me lying under a tree in the middle of the wood which separated the barracks from the headquarter offices. Sick was certainly the right word and my enforced diet for the next 10 days was lettuce leaves and milk. Looking back I now realise I was very close to finishing myself off with a bout of alcohol poisoning.

9

Encounter with a Bluebell Girl

The English lads with me were a great bunch but that didn't stop them giving me a rough ride from time to time. They loved to wind me up and I gave them wonderful ammunition when I let it slip that I was going down into Paris to meet a young relative of my favourite aunt, who was living in Paris. Was she female? Yes. Was she beautiful? I didn't know, we had only met as children. Did Susan know I was going to meet someone of the opposite sex in Paris? Y..y..Yes. So what did she think about it? She understood, I tried to explain, and then let the cat out of the bag by revealing the young lady in question was a Bluebell Girl working at the Lido in the Champs-Elysees. What a fool! I couldn't resist a bit of bragging that would raise my status in their eyes. I could see they were green with envy and was not surprised when they vented their feelings by forecasting an early 'Dear John' or, they all agreed, perhaps it would be the other way round, a 'Dear Susan'.

An early escape was essential and I fled for the bus to the centre of Paris, actually feeling more apprehensive than exhilarated. I counted the trees down the Champs-Elysees and picked out the one we had agreed to meet by (to ease my conscience I kept telling myself I was doing this to please my dear Aunt Wynne, a determined woman with a match-making instinct). I leaned against the tree and took little notice of the tall young woman who seemed to be heading in my direction but could not have been the little girl I had played with many years before. She looked down at me---and I mean looked down--- and asked quite sweetly if I was Corporal John. I looked up and it dawned on me for the first time that Bluebell girls had fabulous legs but were tall...very tall. And I didn't have to remind myself that I never went out with girls who were even one inch taller than myself, let alone five. The conversation was polite and she paid for the coffee at one of the very expensive cafes in this famous avenue. Then we shook hands and said good bye... it was pleasant meeting and Aunt Wynne would be very pleased we had made the effort. What that dear lady didn't understand was that on these occasions chemistry is very important and both Marcia and I realised it was conspicuous by its absence. I never did succeed in explaining to the lads back at camp that the meeting had been something of a failure. Some of them undoubtedly thought it was a cover up and probably the afternoon had been more exciting than I had made it out to be. I didn't mind that. All that concerned me was that my wife-to-be was much more attractive than my 'date' and I didn't have to stand on a box to give her a hug.

In 1957 it was still a novelty for young people with little cash to fly and when a notice went up inviting British servicemen to take part in a draw for a seat on the plane of U.S Army Chief of Staff, General Schuyler, who had a speaking engagement in Bristol, I was the first to add my name. I was lucky and started planning for what was to be a magical day. Susan joined my Mum and Dad to meet me off the plane at Bristol's Lulsgate airport. It took less than an hour, a somewhat shorter time than plodding back to the West Country on train, channel ferry and coach. To add to the excitement, there was a Post photographer to meet me at the gangway and a picture of me walking proudly at the side of an American General appeared in that day's edition. While the General was talking to the local branch of the Institute of Directors on NATO Defence Policy, I was having lunch with my parents and fiancé who were having almost as much difficulty as I was in realising I had appeared out of the sky and would be gone again in a couple of hours. Needless to say Mum and Dad gave me a few minutes alone with Susan, brief moments of intimacy which seemed like a dream when I found myself back in the NAAFI having tea.

Another adventure was a hitch-hike to Deauville during a brief leave which did not leave enough time to make the trip home. The thermometer was rising and we set out with little more than a ground sheet and a packet of sandwiches. The early part of the trip went well with a lift that took us almost half way to the coast. A second kind French driver mopped up another few miles but then our luck started to run out.

We spent a night in a field where I was nearly trampled to death by a cow, a frightening experience when it's dark and one's assailant is not distinguishable. In the morning we started to walk in the direction of Rouen and for the rest of the day it was like an army training route march in the heat which had me thinking it would have been more fun staying in the shade of the Bois de Boulogne. Dreadfully tired by this stage and getting wet in a sudden downpour we opted to spend the night under one of the bridges over the River Seine. It was obviously popular with the drop-outs because along one side of the bridge a dozen or more tramps had taken up residence.

Not wild about the possibility of joining them I persuaded my fellow walkers that the opposite side was more appealing and we made ourselves as comfortable as possible with only a ground sheet to lie on. I remember Brian, a fellow corporal, giving me a dig in the ribs and suggesting we angled ourselves more closely to the wall of the bridge to counter the effect of a cold wind whistling through the tunnel. He didn't realise he was saving both of us from a horrible accident. Neither had noticed that embedded in the dockside were train lines, a fact that became apparent when I was awakened by the noise of a goods train which was moving so close to us we could have reached out and touched the wheels. If we had continued to lie with our legs stretched outwards at least one of us would have lost a limb. We knew at that moment why the tramps had occupied positions well away from the rolling stock they knew passed by at frequent intervals. Not one of them had warned us of the peril but then they were probably asleep when we arrived!

With the help of an early morning milk truck we did arrive in Deauville eventually but the driver was able to explain why getting a lift on that piece of road was virtually impossible. Most of the cars were on their way to the Deauville casino and the drivers with their loaded wallets were not going to stop for anyone.

The weather improved and we were able to enjoy the delights of the beach at Deauville. The return jaunt was without incident and we were back in time to take up duties in our respective offices; if our lifts had been few and far between we might have finished up in the guardroom. My calendar of dates was starting to get thinner as I feverishly tore of the numbers day by day but I now had to admit that this period in the French capital had not turned out to be as bad as I anticipated it might have been. There was never likely to be another time in life when I would be given the freedom to explore the capital of another country without the restrictions which apply on a short holiday. True everything was done within the confines of a pretty miserable budget but it was amazing what could be achieved with a little ingenuity…even a visit to places like The Louvre. But it needed time and practice to get the most out of Paris on a national serviceman's wage not designed for riotous living. Occasions for an exuberant party were usually created by a brave individual who wanted to celebrate his pending demobilisation by kicking over the traces. The Latin Quarter cafes known for serving huge tankers of 'brun formidable' (very strong German beer) laid the foundations and as darkness closed in huge packets of cheap soap powder appeared from nowhere. The contents finished up in the fountain at the edge of the quarter and the suds formed a mountain that was dense enough to stop the traffic. One or two of the more careless servicemen spent an uncomfortable night in the basement of a French gendarmerie but in time the gendarmes, while not exactly joining in the fun, did come to accept it as a harmless event which did much less damage than a riot by French students.

As the days ticked away, ever closer to the final ripping off of the last segment of my calendar, we were allowed to spend more of our time in civvies, dumping the ghastly khaki uniform into any available space in the bedside lockers. By this time friendships had been formed with men of all nationalities and it was not unusual to call an Italian sergeant by his first name, frowned upon, of course, by his British counterpart. Another accepted drift from the rules was to use ones identity card to visit the security area on the pretext of picking up some personal item left on a desk in the restricted area. It so happened that a line to the Ministry of Defence in London was kept open and the bravest among us would pick up the handset and be immediately connected to the MOD operator. 'Which department do you want?' was the question and while endeavouring to sound very official I would request to be put through to a number in Bath. It was a gamble whether a friendly operator had been located and whether the next voice on the line would be mother, father or girl friend. The operator was quite aware, of course, that rules were being broken but most of them turned a blind eye. In the 1950s a call from Paris to Bath by normal channels might well have worked out at £3 a minute. Someone had decided that the poor British national serviceman needed a perk or two. This was one of them, unofficial though it may have been.

10

'Back on the boat again…farewell to France.'

When 'demob' time arrived it was necessary to return to Aldershot to be officially discharged. Not, one might have thought, a pleasing experience, but spirits were high and the uniforms that had been treated contemptuously for many months looked ready for the rag and bone man rather than being handed back into military stores. However, it still had corporals' stripes on the sleeve meaning that the regimental policemen who would have loved to continue their reign of terror started 20 or so months previously could only look on helplessly as we flaunted our short but exhilarating moments of freedom. It was fun wandering around the camp for a couple of days with everything creased and unpolished and smiling at the furious expressions of the regulars who considered we were something the cat had brought in. All of it---uniform, caps, belts and boots---went back into store and probably came out for the next unfortunate squad of trainees without so much as a good brush down. Two intakes later national service for English lads came to an end.

Much to the surprise of many my engagement to Susan had survived and we were, we felt, living proof of the old saying that 'absence makes the heart grow fonder'. Long before my discharge in November 1958 we had started planning our wedding and caused tremors in the family by saying we were not going to wait a moment longer than January 3. Every objection in the world was raised, including the fact that there would probably be snow on the ground and no one would be able to travel. One objection that couldn't be levelled at us was that 'we were rushing into things.' My father, not too seriously, forecast that our marriage wouldn't last longer than a couple of years. But his opinion might have been coloured by the fact that the divorce rate in Britain was increasing at an alarming rate.

I anticipated getting my Bath job back but had to spend a few weeks in Bristol shaking off the lazy habits of an army existence. It was not easy but the sub editors now treated me with a little more respect. They had liked a couple of features I had written about SHAPE and about Paris at Christmas time and they sympathised with me for being allowed a miserly day or two off for my honeymoon. It was a very small wedding because there was little money in either family purse and we wanted to spend what there was on making a good start to our married lives. It was frosty but the snow stayed away and a number of very kind relatives and friends turned up at Saltford Church, near Bath undeterred by the fact that they had not received an official invitation. Even my dear Aunt Wynne braved the elements to travel by road from London and from all accounts did not grind her teeth at the sight of Susan at my side rather than her favourite niece, Marcia, the Bluebell girl.

After a small lunch-time reception at the Lansdown Grove Hotel, Bath, we set off on what was to be one of the shortest honeymoons on record---three days in a London Hotel that my father had recommended and booked for us. What a mistake that was. Allowing him to make the booking, I mean. He wasn't known for being a practical joker--- perhaps because he never had the time--but he certainly stitched up that hotel in a way we would never forget. Young people forming their relationships in today's free and easy climate probably wouldn't appreciate the significance (and joy) of a honeymoon. So many couples live together for years, allegedly seeking to find out how well they might get on under the same roof, that travel plans following the ceremony can hardly be thought of as anything other than a holiday, hopefully a special one. So our experience of arriving at the Berners Hotel in central London and being shy about walking into a bedroom together is likely to sound positively quaint, if not a touch naïve. In the room was a single bed and not a very wide one at that so I had to screw up courage and complain to reception that we had ordered a double room with a double bed. A move was negotiated but the assistant manager insisted that the man who made the booking asked for a single room. It didn't occur to us that perhaps someone had played a prank on a couple of newly weds until there was a knock on the door at 6.0am and a waitress walked boldly into the room with our 'ordered' early morning tea. Light was beginning to dawn and when we were surrounded by waiters wanting to help us put the milk on our cereal, we smiled through gritted teeth and told them we would like to be left alone. We never proved anything but we advised all our friends on the threshold of marriage to be careful how much information they divulged to their families and friends...especially to their fathers or brothers.

There was no special treatment for me when I got back to the office; newspapermen are not known for their romantic traits and my first diary job involved trudging across Bristol to report on the prize-giving at one of the lesser-known public schools. It had not been forgotten that Bath City Football Club had been my territory and I was despatched to Colchester where the team was drawn away in a first round FA cup match.

The Bath line-up was impressive with names like Mortensen, Fleming, Skirton and Book (later player and manager at Manchester City) but they could not weave the magic needed to beat a football league club. Bath returned home nursing a 2-0 defeat.

Almost everywhere in my collection of scrap books I find stories which demonstrate how much life has changed over the last 50 years. I had to warn the Bristol public that the chances of getting a cheaper turkey for Christmas by leaving it until the last minute was not going to work in 1959. The reason? Poultry farms said that they would no longer be 'giving away' their goods during the last few days before Christmas because advanced forms of refrigeration were now working in their favour. The Post Office announced that the postage of a Christmas card in an unsealed envelope, weighing under two ounces, would still be two-pence as long as the card contained no more than the name and address of the sender and recipient and a conventional greeting not exceeding five words! Another 'how life has changed' headline appeared at about this time. A vicar obviously feeling passionate about changing attitudes to this important Christian festival urged his congregation to think more seriously about the celebrations they were planning with an entreaty that ---*'Christmas was not just an excuse to go gay.'* No one even blinked!

To my relief, I was allowed to return to Bath, the city where despite a rocky introduction I had started to make something of my life as a journalist. While I was 'suffering' the delights of Paris, a good chum John Donaldson had been persuaded to look after the Bath office but opinions on his performance were divided. He was one of the best at digging out a story but like many reporters of that time he was over fond of his regular pint of Worthington E. Regular meant three pints at lunch-time and maybe four or more later in the day. So as often as not a good story gathered with great skill stayed in an over-crowded notebook and unless eased out of him by an understanding colleague, never made it to its rightful place on the front page. John was not surprised when the job he had been doing with varying degrees of success was handed back to me. He turned freelance and for several years we had a very good working relationship---he unearthed many excellent stories and on several occasions I did the rest. Such an arrangement made sure that his version, if it appeared in the national newspapers, was never better than the one that went to Bristol. And it also meant I had an ally in my battle with the Bath Chronicle.

Over the years Bath had been one of the most newsworthy cities in the country. Good stories seemed to drop into my lap on a weekly basis but it was still necessary to spend time on cultivating the switchboard operators of the fire, police and ambulance services. I always had an ample flow of tips on fires, car crashes and attempts to rescue pet tabbies from the tops of tall trees but this meant suffering the over keen operator who would call me in the small hours and have me heading out into the countryside to report on a haystack fire. Try as I did to cultivate the news sense of local firemen, I never managed to get them to be more selective about their middle of the night calls. It was another of the penalties of being a lone reporter but there were times when a disturbed night was well worth while.

One of these occasions was a blaze at the Regency Ballroom, once a variety theatre before bingo and discos became all the rage. The fire had started in the early hours and had not been spotted in time to save any part of the ballroom. When the brigade arrived the blaze was about to break out into rooftops of surrounding buildings, threatening an inferno that would have eclipsed anything the German bombers had managed to do. The danger was that the whole of Westgate Street with its shops, offices, hotel and a cinema would be wiped off the map. When the fire chief later showed me the inside of the ballroom, I remarked on the fact that all the ashtrays were still on the tables. When he invited me to touch one, it disintegrated into a little pile of powder an indication of how intense the heat had been.

The blaze destroyed the building just seven days after a successful take-over bid but it was to make an amazing comeback in the mid sixties. A loophole in the licensing laws allowed the ballroom operators to offer all night jazz and pop sessions once a month. When most people were thinking of going to bed a crowd of up to 1000, most of them aged 15 to 25, piled into the ballroom. They paid ten shillings each to spend eight claustrophobic hours listening to non-stop jazz. The Bristol news editor didn't have the nerve to insist I saw the all-night rave through to its bitter end. But he wanted me there early morning to interview the hardy few who had stayed the course! Those who survived were quick to mock the less energetic who gave in around 3.0am and fell asleep slumped against the walls. The Regency attracted its fair share of big names over the years including Georgie Fame, The Kinks, Cilla Black and Sounds Incorporated but these were more civilised affairs.

Across the road from the former Palace Theatre was the gracious Theatre Royal which escaped the blaze and continued to provide the city with live entertainment of a somewhat higher standard. Much of it was repertory theatre in the 50s and 60s but its annual pantomime was rated as one of the best in the country and still is. One of my favourite shows as a child, chosen for an annual treat rather than the pantomime, was a show called 'Twinkle' hosted by Clarkson Rose. This piece of good old fashioned family entertainment was a favourite in Bath for many years. For the more sophisticated there were plays with some well-known actors in leading parts, among them Evelyn Laye, Frank Lawton, Ciceley Courtneidge, Nora Swinburne. Jack Warner, Claude Hulbert and Dennis Price.

My inexperience as a critic was highlighted when I went back stage to interview Jessie Matthews, who was coming near to the end of a long theatrical and musical career. I made the mistake of suggesting she was making a come-back. 'Come-back, come-back!' she screamed, 'I've never been away.' She didn't toss me out of her dressing room but I believe she was on the point of doing so. Jessie proved her point when she went on to play a leading role in the popular radio programme 'The Archers'. All this may sound very exciting but the bitter truth was that I had to write my theatrical reviews overnight for next day's editions. After a hectic week and weekend I was so tired I often struggled to put two words together. One night I was found asleep across my desk by a Post director who had seen the office lights on after a visit to the Theatre Royal. His genuine concern about the pressure I was working under probably prevented me having a nervous breakdown.

Another example of how popular the Royal family was in the 50s came when Princess Alexandra visited the city to inspect 3,500 Red Cross cadets from Somerset, Gloucestershire, Cornwall, Devon, Wiltshire and Bristol. She flew into the Colerne R.A.F. station and the roads all the way into Bath were lined with welcoming crowds. At the Guildhall a gathering of well over 10,000 watched the Princess arrive and one of the problems was where to park 82 coaches arriving from all over the south west to bring cadets for the afternoon inspection.

11

Menuhin, the Beatles and Princess Margaret

On my return from Paris it gave me great pleasure to find that the Bath Festival of Arts had recovered from previous financial problems and the organisers, helped by having the violinist Yehudi Menuhin as its king-pin, was preparing for a spectacular event in June 1959. He had invited his two sisters Hephzibah and Yalta to take part in a Mozart concert, the first time the three members of the family were to play together. It was this sort of innovation which gave the festival a new lease of life and was equalled only by a later invitation to the French jazz violinist Stephane Grappelli to join him in a unique Theatre Royal concert. Needless to say tickets became very hard to get. To persuade the people of Bath to become more deeply involved, all sorts of extravagant fringe events were held and the most memorable of these were a Roman Orgy in the Roman Baths, an Italian event (La Serenissima) in the Parade Gardens and a dance on the platform of the disused Green Park railway station. More about these later.

When the rains fell Bath was always in the front line for a spell of serious flooding and just as Christmas was looming in 1960 the waters rose with vengeance. Later the City was to get an expensive flood protection scheme but in December 1960 there was nothing to stop the city being swamped by the dirty waters of the River Avon. Eventually only one main road out of the city was completely free of water. It happened at about the time another newspaper, the Western Daily Press, had joined the Bristol United Press stable but no one thought of sending a second reporter to Bath to meet the very different and complex demands of two publications. As soon as I had signed off for the day for the Post, the phone started ringing again and the morning paper wanted me to produce follow-ups that were fresh and packed with new information. You could not fault the energy and keenness of Eric Price who had left Fleet Street with a brief to revitalise the ailing WDP but he made no allowances for the fact that he was doubling my already extraordinary workload. He decided early in the proceedings to make the flood story his page one lead but he didn't want any of the material, dramatic as it was, that had already been used in the Post so to my wife's extreme annoyance he rang her at 1.0 am to ask why he still hadn't received new copy. Icily, Susan told him if he went to the Lower Bristol Road he would probably find me in a rowing boat talking to people trapped on the upper floors of their homes. It has to be said that Price did my story real justice on the front page but Susan, bless her, didn't think it necessary for him to ring again at 5.0am to congratulate me on a job well-done. Price was that sort of fellow; about to leave the office he thought it a nice gesture to congratulate one of his reporters before he went home to bed. Little thought, though, for those he was disturbing.

The Pavilion, a barn of a place used for roller skating and big pop concerts, was the venue for one of the first provincial concerts by the Beatles and they arrived in the city at the time teenage hysteria was beginning to mount. In fact they had only three hits to their name when they visited Bath in 1963 and could really be said to be cutting their teeth. Across Bath teenagers begged their parents to let them see their heroes and on a hot June evening the queues formed hours before the concert was due to start. It was the one time in my career I actually gave a story a little extra boost by spreading information that the group were staying at the Francis Hotel in Queen Square. My 'rumour' quickly spread and this sedate part of Bath was inundated with excited fans. It made good pictorial coverage for the cameramen who were already in the city for the concert. The hotel manager was not so pleased.

An even bigger focus of attention in the 60s were the 'goings-on' at Widcombe Manor, the home of entrepreneur and inventor Jeremy Fry, who was described in the Times as a man who trod a fine line between the risqué and the scandalous. Princess Margaret and Tony Armstrong-Jones were frequent visitors to the Manor and Fry was to be best man at their wedding until it became known that he had a conviction for homosexuality. My ex Fleet Street editor Eric Price loved this story and frequently disturbed my night's sleep so that I could patrol the lanes around Widcombe Manor especially on a Sunday morning. The official line was that they were attending communion in the local church which they did on several occasions. Eric was more interested in what they had done the night before and it was this type of snooping that I found distasteful. There were, of course, members of Fry's staff who were happy to report on the riotous parties but money didn't pass hands on a scale to become the norm a decade or so later. Tit-bits like the fact that Jeremy had created a private suite for the engaged couple equipped with its own juke box always commanded premium space in the WDP. The local police did their best to stop cameramen and reporters following the Princess's car but despite the very narrow lanes around the Manor they often failed. Long range camera lenses had recently become a favourite tool and it was not difficult to record interesting activities from the surrounding wooded area. I was one regional reporter who breathed a big sigh of relief when eventually the best man issue was resolved and the couple went off to get married well away from the West Country.

One event they did make a point of attending was the Bath Festival and it was not just the arts that attracted them. They liked the fringe events as well and there was huge publicity when they decided to attend the 18th century Venetian spectacle on the banks of the River Avon---La Serenissima. By this time Eric Price had decided he hated the Bath 'set' and decided to throw oil on a fire that kept the rivalry between the two cities well alight. As usual I was covering the event for both the Post and the WDP and two versions were required even though it meant me staying up the whole night to fulfil this mission. I played it straight for the Post but was ordered by Price to give the event plenty of stick. His excuse was that in his opinion it was yet another event for the snobs and the locals were just spectators. For the only time in my journalistic career I was given an instruction to write a story which justified the headline already penned by the editor---**SNOB SERENISSIMA.** He obviously felt I had defied his orders because what I saw next day was a complete re-write of my original copy.

He did get a good follow up, however, because I felt I could not ignore the fact that entire flower beds in the Parade Gardens had withered. Huge volumes of the event's special cocktail, Venetian Moonlight, had been scattered which did not surprise one guest, my father, who followed his policy of never drinking anything not clearly identified. Next day the odour in the gardens was still mighty strong and I have always maintained that mentholated spirits might well have been one of the ingredients, never proved I have to admit. But I was able to provide an interesting footnote to this story. One female VIP was said to have lost her false teeth in the River Avon but my informant could not be persuaded to name names.

My cavalier editor was not around for another controversial event, a Roman Orgy in the Roman Baths, which was a splendid affair but would certainly have incurred his displeasure. Scantily dressed, attractive young girls swam around in the steaming mineral waters of the baths carrying grapes on silver dishes and gave great pleasure to the toga dressed males waiting for the fruit and Roman delicacies, including fried dormice, nightingales' tongues and sows' udders. It was all arranged by a colourful and inventive hostess, Barbara Robertson, who for a while was chairman of the Bath Fringe events committee and clashed with Menuhin who thought her activities did nothing for the reputation of the festival. Barbara Robertson was credited with being responsible for more rollicking occasions in the city of Bath than anyone since Beau Nash but there were others apart from the world famous violinist who were not pleased. Scandal was never very far away and the last straw came when at the end of the Roman Orgy people refused to leave at 4.0am and the organisers were forced to drain the baths. I was allowed to go back the next day to witness the clean-up but even now think it best to leave the list of items found at the bottom of the baths to the imagination. Barbara Robertson, born a Fry and a member of the Fry chocolate and cocoa family, married Charles Robertson, heir to James Robertson and Sons, the jam makers, who gave the world the famous gollywog motif. They lived at another of Bath's lovely country buildings, Combe Hay Manor. Barbara Robertson never regretted staging some of the most unusual events, which included a Cave Rave at Cheddar Gorge. Guests were invited to dress in animal skins. 'Bath tends to be a bit stodgy,' she said, 'so we decided to liven it up a bit.' There were other less raucous events such as the use of an abandoned railway line to stage a variety of lively parties at points along the line. This was probably the least ambitious (or one could say less crazy) ventures and did not command the attention other fringe events had done.

Another more respectable festival event, demonstrating how dramatically the cost of living has risen, was a ball in the beautiful surrounding of the city's Pump Room. It promised to be one of the most lavish events the city had ever staged but the cost of tickets worried one member of the festival committee. He feared that the outlay would limit the numbers of citizens likely to attend. The cost? A paltry £2. For that the guests were going to see reincarnations of Beau Nash, Sarah Siddons, Ralph Allen and John Wood who were also making 'appearances' at a production 'Welcome to Bath' staged in the open air by the Bath Drama Club.

These were grand times for Susan and I who were regularly invited to other lively Pump Room events like the Police Ball, The Firemen's Ball as well as a wide variety of social functions that received much more publicity in those days than they do today. With two newspapers to service, just how we managed to keep going is something we marvel about to this day. Still a newly married man in my twenties, I can claim to have had the most varied, exhausting, exhilarating and largely enjoyable training of any journalist in the land.

Remains of the Francis Hotel in Queen Square. The small shop run by John's grandparents and later to become his home is 200 yards away in Chapel Row. The church in the background is where John sang in the choir and where his sister was married. (Photograph Bath Chronicle).

John's father in his National Fire Brigade uniform.

John with sister Ann. Even in war-time parents liked to have family portraits.

John (second left) with National Service colleagues and an American general on a flying visit to Bristol.

John with his wife Susan attending an Elizabethan Feast in King's College, Cambridge.

John receiving a National Press Award from Prince Charles

I don't want to be an ass about it, everyone — but do you really think I'll be all right on the night?

A cartoon which appeared in the Cambridge Evening News to illustrate John's account of his first stage appearance.

John takes to the stage again as Grieg in the 'Song of Norway'.

This Daily Mail feature was a boost for the Keep Sunday Special Campaign.

12

From the Sublime to the Ridiculous

There was something in the air at Bath that simply seemed to keep the stories coming. And there was nothing mundane about them. The repeated theft of milk from the doorsteps of people living on Combe Down, a village community at the top of Ralph Allen's Drive, didn't seem to have great possibilities for a hungry reporter who relished human dramas capable of enthralling a nation. But it turned out to be the opening sequence of a story that kept filling the columns day by day. These were low- key thefts which didn't take up too much of police time and seemed in no way linked to a raid on an electrical shop in the centre of town where goods worth hundreds of pounds were stolen. That was until a dishevelled, hermit-like character was spotted carrying a large object through the entrance of one of Combe Down's notorious disused mines. These mines were formed when stone was extracted by Ralph Allen and others to create Georgian Bath but no one bothered to fill them in on the grounds that it would have been a waste of time and money. When police eventually decided to enter the mine they found an extraordinary amount of stolen goods neatly stacked in one of the caves. The hermit-like character was now prime suspect but how and why he managed to get his haul to the top of one of the city's steepest hills was a mystery police and media desperately wanted to solve. Electrical items were not going to survive very long in such damp and unforgiving surroundings.

The unravelling of this mystery gave me one of my major victories over the Bath Chronicle. Their reporter was also in court when 'the caveman', as he became known, made an appearance charged with stealing the goods found buried deep inside the mines. He never explained why he had gone to all that trouble but far more interesting was the background of this sad character, an aspect of the story that did not seem to interest the Chronicle. The 'caveman' came from a respected local family who had served the city in various ways and his sister spoke of him as a generous brother who didn't smoke or drink. Always keen to improve himself he took a job with a multiple firm of chemists but then decided to pursue his ambition to become a professional photographer. To further this aim he started to build up a collection of valuable photographic equipment. His sister explained that he had become very keen on a local girl but when things started to go wrong he cut himself off from the rest of world.

A county court action resulted in bailiffs entering his flat and he resented their interference. He lost his temper and was given a short gaol sentence. From then on things went from bad to worse. With help from his sister and friends, I was able to write a sad but I hope sensitive piece about his decline but what caught the eye of readers was a photograph of Lawrence Say when he was best man at a friend's wedding. Along side the photograph of him in rags and with unruly hair and beard, it was difficult to believe one was looking at images of the same person. I would have loved to interview that man but after another period in gaol he finished up in a mental hospital. Today one would like to think he would have been given much more sympathetic treatment once he had served his sentence.

Combe Down was again in the news when four young lads from Monkton Combe School decided to spend their day off exploring the mines. They disappeared and because of the extent of the mines and their dilapidated state all the alarm signals started to sound. The boys had left no trail so emergency teams found themselves facing a maze of tunnels some of which were supported by centuries-old wooden supports. Just when everyone was thinking the worst must have happened--- the children injured or cut off by a roof fall---news was relayed to the rescuers that the boys had been found in a garden a mile or so away from the spot where they had set out on their precarious expedition. The owner of a Combe Down house had been somewhat surprised when four earth-spattered little heads bobbed up in the middle of his vegetable patch. This was the happiest of happy endings to a story. The leader of the 'gang' remembered that one of his teachers, who regularly searched for fishing bait, had explained that worms always lived near the earth's surface. The frightened boys were sitting in a huddle wondering if there was anything they could do to save themselves when a worm fell from a crevice above their heads. Bright as buttons and now full of hope they attacked the roof above their heads and were very relieved when daylight could be seen. This was a story to relish but no one could have imagined then that the mines would be back in the news 40 years later for a very different reason (see appendix).

I was too busy to worry my head about office politics back at headquarters but there were developments afoot in the early sixties which would have a profound effect on my life. Although he had limited editorial experience and little idea of how to cope with personnel problems, Richard Hawkins, the managing director's son, became editor of the Bristol

Evening Post. Protected by the 12-mile gap between Bath and Bristol, I didn't have to witness the turmoil this appointment was about to cause. Richard loved classical music and journeyed to Bath to write reviews on concerts and other events he considered too cultural and upmarket for a humble district reporter to concern himself with. But although he was now editor of one of the newspapers I served he avoided me like the plague. I was aware that he didn't get on well with my father and this was thought to be due to the close relationship our two fathers shared. My Dad had moved up the administrative ladder, to Circulation Manager, with an incredible record of increasing the sales of both newspapers, and Richard---what shall I say after all this time---didn't like the influence he thought Ted Alexander had over the chairman of the Bristol Evening Post, W.A Hawkins (like a lot of men in those sort of positions he was known by his initials W.A).

I gathered there was some discontent in Bristol as Richard started to throw his weight about. I was not in a position to study what was happening but I started to feel the first waves of radical change when I was told a young public-school educated boy, with virtually no experience, was being sent to the Bath office to supplement the reporting staff. Having been refused any sort of help for so long I was astounded but started to think that at long last I would have some time to myself. Susan and I wanted to start a family and an eager young help-mate in a news-drenched city might be just the sort of back-up I needed. Oh dear! What a shock was in store. John White was not a young man who had come to work with someone with a fair amount of experience in order to learn his trade. He had come with the intention of making a name for himself in the quickest possible time. In doing so he was about to upset nearly every good contact I had built up over several years. The first was my prime contact the Chief Constable, George Nichols. The skies fell in when a story that did not pass over my desk accused the city of Bath of doing nothing about a 'kerb-crawling' problem---men who toured the city in their cars hoping to pick up young prostitutes. In this instance, to accuse the city of turning a blind eye was to accuse the Chief Constable of incompetence and he was not pleased. Bath probably had its prostitutes tucked away somewhere but I was not aware of any problem which affected the public on any sort of worrying scale. I discovered that the story had probably originated from one court case where a defendant was accused of 'kerb-crawling.' The story in the WDP indicated the city had a major problem which the police were doing little to eradicate. The other troubles John White caused are too numerous to mention but relief came when he disappeared and was said to have gone to France. What caused his flight was never determined but I can imagine he might well have got on the wrong side of another city official who was threatening him with legal action.

Just to complicate matters Eric Price was also continuing his feud with the Bath hierarchy which reached such a pitch solicitors defending him took away two or three of the scrap books I had continued to keep. So for a couple of years in the 1960s I have to rely on my memory to continue telling this story. I don't need my scrap book to recall one nasty fight between Price and the Town Clerk, Jared E Dixon. I had produced a perfectly accurate report in which a councillor at a full meeting of the city council had lost his cool and said Bath was becoming a city of deceit and greed. It was a general comment aimed at the sort of policies the city was adopting but Price had a technique whereby he flagged up inside page stories with mini pictures and a caption on the front page. He chose a photograph of the Town Clerk and underneath wrote a simple caption 'city of deceit and greed' (see page 5)'. Mr Dixon rightly claimed that the juxtaposition of his photograph and the quote was a deliberate attempt to besmirch his name and he accused Price of intentional libel. The row petered out eventually but by the time it was settled I had left Bath. My scrap books were never returned.

I soldiered on for a while until in 1963, a day before my father was to be made Circulation Director of Bristol Evening Post Ltd, he collapsed and died. We all like to see the achievements of our parents acknowledged but I still cringe when reading the nauseating front page piece written by Eric Price who claimed him as *his* 'brilliant circulation manager.' True my father had steered the circulation of that newspaper from 14,000 to 45,000 but the two men had never had the sort of relationship which justified the sickly tribute---'the shock of Alex's sudden death, of our sudden loss, is too great for us to write our proper tribute at once. This will appear in tomorrow's WDP.' My Dad would have hated such queasy and insincere words.

I will refrain from making a connection between the death of my father and what happened to me next. But it can be recorded that Richard Hawkins decided I had been in the Bath job too long---I was getting too close to my contacts, he said, which was not healthy---and sent me off into the wilds of north Somerset to dig out stories in places like Radstock, Midsummer Norton, and Paulton as well as villages between Bath and Bristol such as Keynsham and Saltford. He appointed a colourful character from the east of England, Eddie Duller, who was to take over my Bath job. I didn't realise it at the time but this man was going to have a considerable impact on my life.

13

In Search of Fresh Pastures

But before the changes took place there was to be more drama in Silver Street, the head office of the Post. Richard Hawkins, who had followed a succession of very sound, old-school editors suddenly decided to take off without giving any reasons for his sudden departure. Information was slow to reach me out in the wilds of Somerset but I was told he had gone to France. This was a strange coincidence because John White, the young reporter who had made my life a misery and lost me a number of my best contacts, had also gone to France. Because of the distance between me and headquarters I never had a full account of what had happened but by any stretch of the imagination it was not normal practice for editors with a reputation to protect to up sticks and simply disappear.

I was loathing my job in an area of Somerset where little happened but realised there was only one way to release myself from endless meetings listening to local councillors and officials arguing with each other---to leave and find another job. In the end I didn't have to try too hard. Eddie Duller, seen by a previous boss as a potential news editor, was offered a job back in East Anglia and the Bath Office job became vacant again. To my surprise it was handed back to me without any explanation, a development which didn't seem possible following all the skulduggery of the previous few months. It was conveyed to me along the grapevine that W.A Hawkins, annoyed by the behaviour of his son, had been behind the decision to reinstate me in a job I had always carried out conscientiously and with a fair degree of success. Looking back I should have been grateful but my pride and a growing feeling that it was time for a move anyway made it an easy decision to follow Eddie and take up a challenging position as chief reporter on the Cambridge Evening News. Only Susan stood in the way. She was now mother to our first son, 18-month old Adrian, and didn't want to leave the city in which she had been born and in which she had many relatives and friends. The tendency to leave one's home town and seek better employment elsewhere in the country was only just taking root and she did not see herself as one of the pioneer Mums prepared to follow her husband to new pastures without protest.

I left Bath at a time when great changes were about to take place. The plans for a university (originally classed as a College of Science and Technology) were at an advanced stage and there was talk of the population of Bath increasing by 17,000 which would include 5000 students. But Bath was not to become a university city without a great deal of opposition from the locals as well as from Bristol. When the bulldozers moved onto the Norwood playing fields, High Court Action was threatened and the earth moving machines were withdrawn. One accusation was that the purchase of the land, regularly used as playing fields, had not been legally completed. The public meetings I attended turned out to be some of the most volatile I was ever to experience. There was a large body of opinion that once the university moved into Bath, the city would never be the same. This turned out to be true but many of the changes would be very much to the benefit of the population.

I was not going to be allowed to escape to East Anglia before having to write about the most horrendous accident any reporter or photographer could be called upon to witness; a concrete mixer running out of control down the exceptionally steep Lansdown Road and crushing a family car waiting at traffic lights. The bodies of a couple in the front seats would ordinarily have been removed as quickly as possible but their baby was trapped on the floor at the rear of the car and was still very much alive. The concrete in the mixer was setting and getting heavier by the minute. It was a battle against time. Eventually a crane was able to ease the mixer a few feet off the ground and the baby, covered in her mother's blood, was pulled out unharmed. Emergency workers are trained to cope with such horrors but newspaper reporters are expected to take it on the chin. I have never forgotten that experience and still shudder when I drive to the bottom of Lansdown Road on visits to the city.

In 1964, as I was about to clear my desk, there was yet more drama surrounding the Bath Festival. One big attraction that year was the promised appearance of the ballerina Dame Margot Fonteyn. It was thought she might be joined by Rudolph Nureyev for a spectacular performance in the Theatre Royal. Very expensive tickets sold out quickly but in the end neither appeared. As she prepared for her gala ballet performance, the news was received that her husband, Dr Robert Arias had been shot in a Panama Street. No one was surprised when Dame Margot decided her priority was to fly to Panama to be at the bedside of her husband. The festival organisers were presented with a huge dilemma but appeared to be getting a reprieve when a newspaper headline quoted the ballerina as saying: 'I'll dance tonight'. She had established that after a three hour operation her husband was out of danger. A very relieved Bath Festival Director, Ian Hunter, had been able to tell the press that Dame Margot was determined not to let Yehudi Menuhin and the festival organisers down. But another change of mind gave a final twist to the drama; when the audience arrived at the Theatre Royal there was no Fonteyn and no Nureyev. A very tolerant audience, although disappointed, of course, accepted the situation and instead listened to Menuhin playing the music for the famous solo 'The Dying Swan'. A member of that audience recalled later that listening to the music and 'imagining' Margot's brilliant performance was a poor substitute 'But Menuhin played superbly in a spotlight which went out when the swan died. We all applauded and went home.'

Many challenges had faced the city over the years but one that baffled many experts was what to do with Bath's increasing traffic. The surrounding hills made it virtually impossible to build a by-pass so thoughts turned to a possible underground tunnel. This idea was quickly shelved when it was pointed out that beneath many of the Georgian houses were cellars that could cave in if there was too much below ground level activity. One of the country's top experts Prof Colin Buchanan was called in and he launched the most comprehensive traffic and development surveys ever undertaken outside London. A team of students were marshalled and were briefed to visit 1,500 homes seeking information about the movements of householders and their families. Bath had still not solved its traffic problem 50 years later.

Susan may have been apprehensive about leaving her home town but deep down so was I. The story told in the family is that Sue and I were born in the same Bath maternity home but as there were six months between us there was no question of us having made each others acquaintance at the time. The fact was, however, that we were dyed-in-the-wool Bathonians and I had the accent to prove it. My wife who had attended the Bath High School with such notable women as barrister, Naomi Lethbridge, actress, Barbara Leigh Hunt and cooking celebrity Mary Berry, spent a lot of her time practising the art of ballroom dancing which may explain her lack of desire for academic qualifications. It remains a mystery why she left the school to develop skills as a shorthand typist but perhaps she was destined to help out a teenage reporter who haunted her in the vicinity of Bath Guildhall on a daily basis.

14

And so to Cambridge

Driving across country into the heart of East Anglia was almost as traumatic as crossing the United States in a camper van. We were heading into a flat wilderness and the first shock was to discover how unfriendly Cambridge people seemed to be, at least on the surface. We stopped for a pub lunch on the outskirts of the city and on leaving, walked away from the bar with a cheerful acknowledgement of the food and the service to be met with blank stares from the landlord. It took a few years to accept that Cambridge people did not demonstrate their bonhomie in the manner of the West Countryman. Eddie and his wife Vilma had agreed to give us a roof over our heads while we made final decisions about a new home and where it should be. A lasting memory was how cold it was in the winter of 1964/65, central heating was not an automatic addition to many houses and that coupled with the east winds blowing directly from Siberia did little to cheer our hearts in the early stages of our relocation. Having searched the area for a suitable house without immediate success I travelled back to Bath on a regular basis but then left Sue and Adrian in the home we were still trying to sell. That meant a number of long, lonely journeys before we were able to call up the furniture removal van and make our move permanent.

Editor of the Cambridge Evening News was Keith Whetstone, charismatic and driven by a desire to turn a very dull little regional newspaper into a publication with plenty of spunk. Eddie, who had worked with him before, was to be one of his front line troopers but Eddie knew he was limited in what he could do if anchored to the news desk. The reporting team contained some talent but was basically idle and lacking in news-sense. I was to be the man who was going to kick some life into them by dragging them away from their telephones and exposing them to the outside world. It was an uphill task to begin with because they had never worked for a chief reporter who would not take 'no' for an answer. His habit of sending them back to the source of an inquiry if they returned to the office empty handed and with a string of excuses never went down well especially if they had to cancel a planned night out.

Early in our relationship they were convinced I was mad when I insisted we should stay on the tail of a group of bird fanciers who were distressed by the disappearance of a rare parrot from a Cambridge public house. Perhaps I would not have been quite so keen if it had not been the 'silly season' when news of any kind was in short supply. It was, however, an example of a story that if pursued enthusiastically and reported with tongue in cheek could keep a large percentage of a newspaper's readers transfixed. This only became clear to some of the younger reporters when they overheard the future fate of Polly being discussed by passengers on the top of a bus. The story came to a head when a group of bird lovers, on being told that Polly had been seen in a tree at a local park, concocted an enticing supper---the sort that parrots were thought to be particularly fond of--- and sat for part of the night at the base of the tree waiting for the hungry bird to be lured to the ground. It worked and the next day's front page photograph was of Polly happily entertaining customers in the smoky atmosphere of the Queen Edith lounge bar once again. Nobody pretended it was a world shattering story but it did prove to a bunch of Eddie's would-be newshounds that persistence and a little imagination pays off. The young reporter who took his chance and woke me up in the middle of the night to report a UFO over Cambridge (the incident referred to at the start of my story) continued to display initiative but was as surprised as I was when Polly's story was reported in newspapers around the world.

After years in the job, newspapermen generally come to the conclusion that nothing is really new. But the barrage balloon incident had no precedent and also caught the imagination of people in other countries. Balloons, used at weather stations, may still break away from their mooring from time to time but are unlikely to cause the havoc Cambridge experienced that night. One statistic we should have gathered but didn't, was how many people were taken to the city's hospital with suspected heart attacks.

It is difficult to believe that in 1966 a reporter still had to queue up at a telephone box to file the details of a story back to his office. This all changed when Pye Telecommunications Ltd, based in Cambridge, launched a new range of radio-telephone. The news that the Prime Minister had armed himself with a Pye pocket radio-telephone received plenty of attention and at the invitation of Pye, newsmen climbed aboard a London double-decker bus and filed their stories back to their offices without any problems. Until this time the Pocketfone with a range of up to five miles had been used mainly by the police and emergency services. Life was never going to be quite the same ever again. There were plenty of innovators in Cambridge and one who constantly found himself in the news was Clive Sinclair, who had not had great success with his miniature car but looked more likely to succeed with the world's smallest and cheapest television set. The company, Sinclair Radionics, had from the outset specialised in the development of miniaturised electronic equipment and claimed to be growing bigger because it was 'thinking smaller' than everyone else.

The most reliable providers of zany stories in Cambridge were its university students so no one was particularly surprised to wake up one morning to find a banner calling for Peace in Vietnam flapping between two spires of King's College. In a daring and dangerous night climb they had taken little more than an hour to shin 147 feet to the top. And then they had the cheek to warn the Dean of the Chapel that unless the stone work was restored the lives of future climbers could be endangered. The college said they knew the stone work needed attention but it was not a priority job. It was fine as long as people didn't climb about on it.

There was more innovation during the 60s and a story that attracted world attention centred on the city's famous teaching hospital, Addenbrooke's. This time it was a major breakthrough in the field of transplanting human organs. In May 1965 a team of surgeons led by Prof Roy Calne, gave new hope of life to a woman with a fatal liver disease. In a six hour operation she was given the liver of a person who had recently died. Similar operations had been carried out in Denver, Colorado, but this was the first liver transplant operation to take place in Britain. Many have been carried out since and not every patient has survived but the success rate is such that most people who receive a transplant in the new millennium do expect a lengthening of their lives by an ever increasing number of years.

In some areas of my new job it was business as usual. Council meetings in Cambridge were just as long and were made quite nerve-shattering by an editor who insisted on sitting through the entire proceedings to make sure his reporters didn't miss anything, a sad demonstration of how little confidence Keith

Whetstone had in the troops he had gathered around him. We were still in the typewriter days and he had a disturbing habit of standing behind you when you were writing a story, sometimes making little comments about where you were going wrong. A problem to overcome as far as I was concerned was to create a good, open relationship with the Cambridge police along the lines I had achieved in Bath. Most of the senior detectives felt nothing but contempt for the editorial team and it took me quite a while to convince them that we could be of help to each other if there was a mature attitude to police/press co- operation. One colleague who helped turn things around was a tough, determined Scotsman, Jock Gillespie, who demonstrated his skills when dealing with the complicated and fast moving story involving the infamous Cambridge rapist. He above everyone else convinced the police that they needed the media as much as we needed them. Eddie Duller's role in this drama was such that he achieved national recognition and later became Editor of the Oxford Mail---an unlikely appointment in some respects because Eddie was a tough cookie and not the sort the average Oxford academic would have automatically embraced.

When Keith Whetstone left for another senior editorial position in Coventry, there was the usual speculation about who would step into his shoes. When one of the feature writers found the editor-elect mentioned in Burke's peerage, as son and heir of Lord Hemingford, the knives came out and the prediction was that such a person would go straight into the pockets of the Cambridge elite and as an ex Cambridge man would have a natural bias towards the city's university set. Nothing could have been further from the truth. Nick Herbert, as he preferred to be called, was without doubt one of the best editors operating in the regions. He certainly didn't bow to the university crowd and stood his ground when the National Union of Journalists decided to do battle with him.

Plenty of material appeared under Nick's reign which was very much to the benefit of Cambridge people but he will always be remembered by me for his conviction that a newspaper should also have its lighter side and that was certainly reflected in the improved circulation figures. Some will say they were stunts but they were stunts with a purpose. When a specialist writer described the British bulldog as 'an unworthy symbol of the British Empire---ailing and unable to move a short distance without getting out of breath'--- letters arrived from all parts of the country in defence of this pugnacious animal. The proud owner of a six-year-old bitch offered a 50 yards start to any competitor the writer liked to name. The paper was swamped with complaints from bulldog lovers seeking retribution. Nick invited them to take their pets to the Cambridge City Football ground where some of the county's top athletes would provide the opposition over 80 yards. The two-legged runners scored a convincing victory. It provided me with a hilarious feature accompanied by photographs, not likely to get pride of place at the next local breeders show. But they were fun.

Some of Nick's management team colleagues were not amused when he granted permission for a group of feature writers to stage a fish and chip shop competition. The arrangement, presenting all sorts of organisational difficulties, was to co-opt a team of cyclists, motor cyclists and people fast on their feet to collect a portion of fish and chips from every shop in and near the centre of the city. The CEN boardroom was commandeered and some 30 portions of Britain's favourite meal arrived at roughly the same time. Waiting with forks at the ready were four judges, all with some culinary expertise, and after lively debate the best fish and chip shop in the area was crowned. It did a lot for their business but the complaints from the managing director and other top brass about the smell of fish polluting their boardroom did last a few days. Again it was a fun feature but one which was still being talked about in the new millennium.

The feature I should not have attempted on the assumption that only fools go where angels fear to tread was to record an attempt to abolish my foul smoking habit…..and not just to abolish it but to do so in a very public manner. Each day over a week, I took over a small spot in the News diary column to tell readers how I was getting on. The theory was that if I did it publicly, I would feel dreadful shame if I had to admit failure. Non-smokers no doubt thought it was a waste of newsprint but fellow addicts were either challenged and joined me or stopped their evening newspaper for a week or two! I thought I was doing well but taking away one of the major props of a reporter was almost certain to end in disaster. Like many others, whenever a difficult story had to be completed against a deadline a cup of coffee to the right hand side of the desk and a cigarette on the left hand side were as essential as the typewriter itself. No one raised the health issues until very late in the 20th century. It was not unusual for me to sit with my doctor in his surgery and share a cigarette. Well, not exactly share but you know what I mean. I did abandon the nicotine habit eventually, but not until June 12th, 1982 at 4pm precisely. The house we were living in still has dents in the plaster caused, I am told, by throwing punches at the wall when the withdrawal pangs became too awful to bear.

15

Let Loose in Miami

Now Features Editor, one of the 'perks' offered on a regular basis was a trip to some exotic part of the world organised by a travel company or tourist agency keen to attract British holiday-makers to their particular part of the world. These were spread around to the deserving on most occasions but having never travelled to America I decided to take up a tempting offer to spend a day or two on Miami Beach in the luxurious Fontainebleau Hotel. As usual these offers came at the last minute, usually to fill up an under-booked charter 'plane, so there was little time to think seriously about one's wardrobe. The outcome being that a group of down-at-heel regional English journalists turned up at Heathrow still wearing sports-coats and carrying mackintoshes. An umbrella or two may have been secreted in suitcases. I did decide at the last moment to grab a pair of swimming-trunks, watched with envy by my wife and two sons. Actually they were very good about it expressing between clenched teeth that of course Daddy must have a little holiday from time to time. It was reward for working hard.

With temperatures up in the 90s and a hot tropical wind bending the coconut trees outside, there was an urgent need for a change of wardrobe. Sports coats just had to go, a desire made greater by the sight of Americans on their way to dinner with colourful summer shirts worn, we were told, for one or two days and then binned. The pool just visible from the 14th floor looked very inviting after a long sweaty trip so I undressed, wrapped myself in my quaint summer housecoat, grabbed a towel and headed for the lift. The first of many shocks was about to come. Stepping out of the lift into the basement I found myself in a shopping centre which today might be compared with Lakeside off the M25 but in the 70s was a revelation to a hack journalist who had only seen America, courtesy of the silver screen. I have been embarrassed a few times in my life but walking through an up-market shopping centre in an old housecoat (not even one made of towelling) took the biscuit. In the end I had to stop and ask a well-dressed tourist the whereabouts of the swimming pool. She was most helpful but I could see she was having great difficulty in restraining her amusement. There was no one in the pool---much too early for guests at this hotel said the pool attendant. Totally blown by the time change and my first long flight across the Atlantic, it took me a minute or two to work out what he meant by 'too early.' Mentally, I was still in my English bed and breakfast mode expecting to dash across the prom for an early morning dip, without causing a sensation.

Coping with eating arrangements was the next hurdle because the Miami Tourist Board wanted us to try everything, and I do mean everything---a maple syrup and waffles breakfast, followed by a burger lunch; six or seven burgers stacked and filled so outrageously as to block vision for yards around. And then before the digestive juices had been given a chance to fulfil their function, a bus arrived to whisk a bloated party of Englishmen off to meet the Mayor of Miami at a banquet in another of the opulent waterfront hotels. The steaks (with fries, of course) were massive and I knew I was about to make a fool of myself for the second time. I was saved by the action of the Mayoress who took one delicate chunk out of her steak, chewed it slowly before pushing the plate to one side with the comment that it was 'quite splendid.' No embarrassment on her part that her meal and many others would finish up in the trash can. This example of casual waste was horrific and in a kind of subdued outrage I told her how my mother, taught to cope during the war years, never wasted anything. Left over potatoes and vegetables were turned into bubble and squeak and the remains of the rice pudding stored in the larder for the next day. She said nothing but could not disguise her disgust. It was a unique experience but when my brain cleared, I realised we were being used to encourage the British to take to the air and fill Miami flats and holiday homes during the unbearably hot summer months. We were being entertained in November, the month the Americans start arriving for a winter holiday in the sun. No one from the UK except the very rich would be able to compete with the bulging wallets of our American friends. The Tourist Board was not happy when I pointed this out in my newspaper's travel section. But perhaps they learned that handing out free trips did not always guarantee glowing coverage.

After these few days of indulgence it was back to the grindstone and I knew I had a long way to go with my young team when trying without a lot of success to interest them in the activities of a young Cambridge man who was promoting himself as the Western World's most gifted psychic. Matthew Manning became a regular celebrity in the tabloid press as he set up demonstration after demonstration of so-called paranormal experience. Furniture 'flew about' his parents home in the village of Great Shelford, paintings from the hands of dead artists appeared on his bedroom walls, messages were said to be conveyed to him from famous people wanting to express their opinions from beyond the grave. This was not considered by the more responsible press to be acceptable material and for sometime the CEN stayed firmly on the sidelines demonstrating to the people of Cambridge it was above such things. That was until a respected, retired teacher at Matthew's former school sent me a postcard querying why his ex pupil, in reply to the questions of inquisitive reporters, kept denying he had artistic ability; in his own words was never able to draw a straight line, let alone produce creditable copies of works by the masters. Not only did the teacher remember Matthew had a flair for art work but had actually won an Art Cup at school. He enclosed a school magazine which recorded this fact. It is a magazine that still holds pride of place among by souvenirs. This revelation helped to convince those already sceptical that Matthew was quite capable of producing good copies of famous paintings on his bedroom walls. Experts at the Fitzwilliam Museum in Cambridge were later to endorse this view by acknowledging the skill of the paintings but at the same time pointing out what to them were obvious discrepancies.

Unaware that the game was up, Matthew started to look for new ways of keeping the tabloids interested. Rashly, he decided to exploit a document purporting to name the real killer of President John F Kennedy. If true it would have been an explosive revelation but it had already been written off by most branches of the media as material without any foundation. Journalists around the world had received a copy and all but the blatantly sensational operators relegated it to the spike or at least to the 'no immediate action required' file. Matthew, however, knew nothing about this and decided on a trip to America where with a little manipulation he thought he could boost his paranormal ratings. He would do this by compiling a paranormal message based on the document with the intention of sending it back to his faithful but gullible supporters in Britain. At first the ruse appeared to work but then to everyone's surprise Matthew made a hurried return to Britain and issued a statement that he no longer wished to be known as a psychic. In future, he wanted to be known as 'a mentalist'. It was difficult to come to a conclusion as to what that actually meant. He refused to give any explanation and decided to make himself scarce; leaving unanswered the question of why he had retreated from the States in such a hurry. Some were convinced that there may have been accusations in the Gemstone File (the volatile document containing 'the truth' about Kennedy's death) that were a little too plausible for some people's comfort. Did Manning receive threats which convinced him not to hang around on the other wide of the Atlantic? It was just one of the conspiracy theories to add to the many others floating around at the time. My instinct was to try to track Matthew down again but those around me thought the story had run its course and the Manning family should be left in peace. Consequently, it looked as if the last piece of the jigsaw would never be put into place. What I didn't know then was that another opportunity would come my way and eventually Manning would be seen as a very clever manipulator who could survive for a while no matter how much evidence was stacked against him.

16

A Square Deal?

It is always a delight to put to good use the small amount of power granted to the local journalist, not for oneself, but for readers in no position to fight battles single-handed. I was able to do this with a column labelled '*A Square Deal? 'The News' investigates.* It was one of the first of its kind in the country but was not always popular with the advertising department or local retailers because we were invariably highlighting matters they would have preferred to keep under wraps. When a massive project of transferring to North Sea Gas got under way, the controlling organisation Eastern Gas didn't expect its every movement to come under scrutiny and this wouldn't have happened if officials had got their act together in the first place. But their administration was diabolical and they never anticipated the string of complaints that would land on their doorstep if domestic appliances were not converted promptly and effectively. Customers, left waiting to cook their Sunday lunch, cottoned on to the fact that they were likely to get some attention if they complained to the local newspaper. They were absolutely right; engineers confided in me later that the policy at EG was to give urgent attention to cases where bad publicity was in the offing. But there was an unbelievable succession of complaints, not always about conversion but often about customers being hounded to pay bills they had settled months before.

There was a lighter side to the column. As well as running a competition to find the best fish and chips shop in the city, articles were put together on the quality and price of popular fruits such as strawberries and tomatoes. In one mad moment, right in the middle of a heat wave, we tried to fry an egg on the top of a car which had stood all day in the sun. This proved nothing from a consumer's point of view but it was great fun.

Perhaps the most extraordinary story to come my way was the delicate task of uncovering the fraudulent activity of a man known, among many other names, as Jonathan Wearn. He arrived in Cambridge with the intention of setting up a symphony orchestra, yes a symphony orchestra, not a small string quartet or a brass ensemble and his glib tongue and pleasantly persuasive manner convinced amateur musicians all over the city and beyond to join in this 'brave' musical adventure. But it was not just the many excellent amateur instrumentalists he convinced but also world famous performers like Tamas Vasary and Moura Lympany. Wearn was a consummate confidence trickster and by promising eminent musicians and record companies that the new Cambridge Symphony Orchestra would be the greatest thing since the invention of sliced bread, he managed to run up huge debts he had no hope of repaying. He purchased, and tried to sell grand pianos with the nonchalance of a used car salesman. Difficult as it was to look into the background of a man such as Wearn, it was eventually discovered that he had once posed as a doctor and by forging references even managed to find his way into an operating theatre helping surgeons carry out delicate operations. His modus operandi was amazing; never paying any bills and casually using taxis to take him to and from Heathrow at the orchestra's expense.

To impress local bigwigs and persuade them to part with their money he would arrange a dinner party at his rented home and as guests arrived would be heard playing the opening bars of the Grieg piano concerto.

Later it was revealed that those few bars were all he could play.

He might well have had a longer career in Cambridge if one of his local instrumentalists had not been Alan Rusbridger, then a junior reporter but later to become editor of *The Guardian*. Alan discovered that local musicians were not getting promised expenses, local firms who printed concert programmes were not being paid and record companies were having extreme difficulty in getting the money they were owed for recordings. I joined in the hunt to uncover Wearn's duplicity and discovered that as an undischarged bankrupt he should not have been doing any business on credit. When he decided to disappear, I visited the house he had rented in Huntington Road and found a floor littered with correspondence. The suspicion remains that he was the illegitimate son of a member of the House of Lords. This was one fact we were unable to substantiate in spite of letters and other personal items left lying around which pointed in that direction. He made one appearance in court and bearing in mind his previous activities most people were expecting him to get a prison sentence. But Judge David Wild gave him the equivalent of a slap across the wrist (a fine of £250) and glaring at me in the press box said he thought the local press had made a mountain out of a molehill. The people he had swindled to the tune of £50,000 certainly didn't agree and one printing company struggled to stay in business. Like so many con-men, Wearn had a likeable personality and there were more than a handful of people in Cambridge who thought he had been badly treated.

Life changed dramatically from the time Nick Herbert shocked the editorial team by announcing he would be leaving to join Westminster Press as editorial director. All the earlier doubts about him had been long forgotten and several of us remember him as an editor who trusted his reporters and supported them sometimes to his personal disadvantage.

By comparison, his successor was like a sudden rush of cold water on a winter's morning. Colin Webb, who had started his career with the Portsmouth Evening News arrived on the scene with what appeared to be a brief to keep everyone happy at all costs. That was everyone except me. On his second day, over what I first thought was a welcoming drink in the pub next to the office, he made it quite clear that as I had been short listed for his job our relationship might have its rocky periods.

I thought this was his way of declaring he was the boss and all would work out well in the end but was greatly disillusioned when he stopped me on the stairs to the features department and announced that he had accepted the resignation of Alan Rusbridger on the grounds that he was really 'too good' to stay with a regional newspaper. That may well have been true but I began to fear for an editorial team saddled with a chief so little concerned about holding onto his best journalists. Ironically in 1977, Alan and I were given British Press Awards, Alan a commendation in the Young Journalist of the Year class, myself a commendation in the Provincial Journalist of the Year section. For a while Webb's attitude changed. Although he had kept his distance from the entanglements of the protracted Wearn and Manning investigations, he revelled in being able to attend the award presentations by Prince Charles at the Savoy Hotel, London.

As far as my award was concerned the judges had also taken into account the success of the consumer column and the inquiry into the activities of Matthew Manning, who I later found was working on cruise ships bringing 'healing relief' to elderly passengers.

Even today he still has a website on which he calls himself a psychic, a title he had decided to abandon several years earlier. It was no surprise that he showed little interest in seeing the school magazine that had blown his cover by heralding his Art Prize. Probably, he already had a copy discreetly tucked away.

In the end, the only satisfaction I derived from this discovery was being able to use the information in my first attempt at a novel, '*Spoofed and Spiked*' in which I was able to base my main fictional character on Matthew. It was never going to be a best seller because I had a lot to learn about the difference between producing a short snappy feature and a book with something like 96,000 words between its covers. However, the learning curve experience was invaluable.

And there was one other nice surprise to justify all the hard work I had put into uncovering the deceptions of Matthew Manning. A letter appeared in the 'News' correspondence column which praised the 'careful, unpopular and scrupulous investigation' into the activities of Manning. The correspondent wrote: '*The wave of pseudo-scientific phenomena must be a disturbing feature of contemporary life. I fear that it may also be comparable with the wave of occultist hysteria that swept through Nazi Germany (and Hitler's circle itself) before the victory of totalitarianism in Germany. Let the few courageous voices of journalists like Mr Alexander be heard whenever reason and common sense are flouted. Our civilisation needs them.*'---Philip Ward, Editor of **A Dictionary of Common Fallacies.**

There were times during the late seventies when I was on the point of throwing in the towel. I was now working for a newspaper, known for its award winning journalism in past years, which had lost its cutting edge. The best journalists were leaving on a regular basis in their quest to find publications allowing them to exploit their talents. Anything slightly controversial struggled to get across the sub-editors' table and into the hands of the linotype operators (new technology had yet to arrive). But there were still opportunities to produce 'soft' entertaining features and I fully indulged myself as features editor in a variety of off-the-wall features. The amateur stage in my view was an area where circulation figures could be improved. Local people loved to see their names and faces in newsprint so long as the accompanying information didn't originate from the magistrates court. So whenever the full-time theatre correspondent found he couldn't be in two places at once, I would step in and write a review which would be printed the next day, not as happens now, weeks later or not at all. And I knew the majority of 'amateurs' in Cambridge couldn't wait to read about themselves always hoping, of course, that they would be praised to the skies. I don't think I was ever unfair but I could be scathing about actors who hadn't spent enough time learning their lines or producers who had accepted second best from their performers. On one occasion this type of comment got me into trouble when a reader challenged me with the comment: 'It's all very well for John Alexander to criticise but I bet he has never set foot on a stage.' She was right, of course, but her comment gave me an idea for a feature. I would join a light opera group (I sang in school and church choirs in days gone by) and from the back row of the chorus describe just what it was like to tread the boards. At this stage I didn't know there was a plot to give me a small part and I would probably have run a mile in the opposite direction if I had realised what was afoot.

As my article later described in vivid detail, my first dilemma was to try to overcome nerves which forever haunted me whenever I stepped out in front of an audience. Sawston Light Opera Group (aptly named SLOG for short) was the unfortunate company saddled with a novice of the lowliest order. One of the minor characters had been given the name Kras---'small, plump, always worried, flustered and in a great hurry.' It was a masterly piece of casting but I was not too convinced with assurances that Kras was spelt with a K, not C and had only one S. I stayed the course through rehearsal after rehearsal, quite a strain after a hard day's work in the office, and later produced an article that worked wonders for my notoriety. There was an eye-catching cartoon with the caption: 'I don't want to be an ass about it everyone, but do you really think I'll be all right on the night.' Small part it may have been but Kras had started to invade my dreams like some kind of Frankenstein monster. He was a stupid little character who bobbed on and off the stage like a puppet on a string but if he didn't bob when he was supposed to bob, I knew the talented and seasoned campaigners of SLOG were going to pickle me in aspic. As well as an article which caused great amusement, the personal benefits gained from the experience were immeasurable. My reviews would in future be delivered by someone who had discovered the pitfalls for himself and eventually a man who was terrified about stepping out in front of an audience would gain a degree of confidence. The musical director, David Adams, who was a skilful, sympathetic but resolute teacher, laughingly predicted that I would take a major part one day. Amazingly, he was right but that's another story.

17

Around the World in a Plywood Yacht

Other equally quirky stories invaded the 'News' feature pages while the staff waited for an editor who might consider items with a little more weight. For no other reason than to get an entry in the Guinness Book of Records, Robert Manderson, a leading young tenor in SLOG decided to break a record by singing non-stop for nine hours. Smelling of lemon honey and mentholyptus, aids to a tired voice, he was hoisted into the air by fellow members of the group after singing 60 songs, several of them many times over.

If I was seeking more notoriety, I could have not chosen a better vehicle than King's College Choir. An avid supporter for 51 weeks of the year, I turned on them in the 52nd and for a reason I can barely fathom three decades later, decided that decline had set in. As a lowly member of a local amateur operatic group, I really had no right to suggest to conductor Philip Ledger that a performance of three Handel coronation anthems, including Zadok the Priest, was not up to scratch. Going where angels fear to tread, I wrote that for once the music was not so intoxicating that the discomforts of sitting in King's Chapel went unnoticed. I may have been the one who was intoxicated because I went on to suggest that even the mighty can fall if balance, control and a sense of purpose were temporarily lost. I'm surprised now that I wasn't run out of town. Could it be that I was enjoying a sense of power? Some may have thought so when I described a concert by Julie Felix and friends as a 'night to forget.'

It took place in a sports hall and on this occasion I was probably right to side with an audience that had been badly let down. Only 200 bought tickets in the first place and by the end of the evening less than 100 were still in their seats. A sports hall was not a place to try to create the intimate atmosphere so important to a live performance by a girl of great charm and talent. 'Sorry,' said Julie at a point when the sound system let her down, 'but when I stand away from the speaker I feel I am singing in a morgue.' I never did find out if Julie ever recovered from that horrific experience.

During this time there was one running story which no one complained about. It started when an enthusiastic young sailor, Shane Acton, decided to sail around the world in a plywood yacht, Super Shrimp (affectionately called Shrimpie). It was no bigger than a king-size bathtub. He was given a send-off on the River Cam but no one seriously thought he would get very far once he took on the perils of the Atlantic. Strangely, he was forgotten about, maybe because I had not covered the original story and the reporter who did had left the paper. Shane was so relaxed when he set out he said he would take his time and if he found his paradise island he would probably never return. Interest was reawakened when a letter arrived on my desk which had taken weeks to travel from some remote island in the Pacific I had never heard of. What impressed me was his natural writing ability, beautiful descriptions of the places he had visited which made an even greater impact than his accounts of the amazing challenges he faced navigating an 18ft yacht through perilous waters. I encouraged him to stay in touch and send reports whenever he landed somewhere where a postal service operated. So random was his journey that finding a place where a means of communication existed was a rarity. His despatches posted from all parts of the world often came on crumpled pieces of an exercise book, toilet paper or what ever was handy. Sometimes rolls of film were included exposed, he said, on a camera found on a rubbish tip. The charm and enthusiasm of his correspondence did, I felt, disguise the energy, grit, determination and sailing skills which must have come to the fore to get him through a series of near catastrophes.

Two years after setting out from Cambridge he arrived at the paradise island of Tahiti, now accompanied by a Swiss girl, Iris Derungs, someone with the same spirit of adventure as her rugged, handsome 'captain'. They arrived with 50 pence between them but the story of their courage soon got around and Shane was able to find a job refurbishing a yacht for its new American owner. For the first time he felt he could boast a bit. He made three claims:

- Super Shrimp was the smallest yacht to cross the Pacific with two people aboard.

- Iris was the first woman to cross the Pacific in a boat under 20ft

- Shrimpie was the smallest standard production yacht (unmodified) to have sailed 9000 miles and still be on the high seas.

There were no claims of record circumnavigation times. Shane was well outside any records of that sort, about seven years outside. The fact was that Shane, who had served for five years as a Royal Marine, was not in a hurry; he never had a 'round the world or bust' spirit and always maintained that it was an obsession with speed that got some circumnavigators into trouble. He considered they carried too much sophisticated gear that was much more likely to go wrong than the few simple aids he carried aboard. In his cockleshell he crossed the Atlantic and Pacific, cruised through a lumbering band of whales, fought killer waves higher than his washing prop main mast and survived ship wreck in the Red Sea.

When he arrived back in Cambridge in 1980 after 2,887 days taking a look at parts of the world some people had never heard of, he found a message from Prince Philip, then an Admiral of the Fleet, waiting for him. Shane had met the Prince in Australia in March 1977, near the halfway point in Super Shrimp's round-the-world journey. The Royal visitor actually interrupted the tight schedule of a royal tour to meet Shane and inspect his tiny craft.

Many years later, in 2002, I received a message from a former colleague at the News telling me of Shane's death from lung cancer and suggesting I might like to attend his funeral in the Cambridge Crematorium (Shane was a heavy smoker and even at sea would make cigarettes out of tea bags). There was an extraordinary atmosphere in the crematorium because someone had the idea of playing a recording, not of sacred music but of the waves and wind, a sound that would have been familiar on a daily basis to one of the world's most courageous sailors. It brought back memories of one letter he had mailed from a remote island wondering whether his experiences would bring him closer to an understanding of the meaning of life. As someone who had begun to feel a powerful surge in that direction and had become a Christian, I was upset to hear that despite his closeness to nature for so long Shane had experienced nothing spiritual. In fact, he had requested that no hymns or prayers should accompany the ceremony marking the disposal of his earthly remains. I left the crematorium feeling very sad.

Deprived of the opportunity at this stage of my career to do serious investigative reporting, I continued to find subjects that were relatively harmless as far as the hierarchy was concerned but did keep readers amused. They needed something to lighten their day in inflation-hit Britain so I joined scores of people scrambling for potatoes in a Cambridgeshire farmer's field. He had put up a sign 'Potatoes---pick your own' an attractive proposition at a time when the humble spud was costing almost 20p a pound. I described the experience as something akin to the Eton Wall game. There were no rules, no conduct of behaviour and no referee and certainly no thought that women and children should come first. It was every man for himself. There was one redeeming feature. In true British style everyone queued at the weighing machine and even when it broke down patiently passed the time making polite conversation.

Looking back I think that many of my articles had more than a spattering of arrogance about them. But for some people they touched the right nerve. The 70s became noted for a flood of dubious material on our cinema screens and London theatres were saturated by material which glorified in perverted sex and violence. So on the night that most newspapers chose to review what one critic described as 'the ugliest show in town', I set out with some deliberation to listen to a centenary concert of Bach's B minor Mass in the Albert Hall. David Willcocks, the brilliant but modest Director of Music at King's College, Cambridge, was the conductor and my intention was to reflect on two contrasting events and the attention they attracted. I commented that in seedy London this celebration concert, although not to everyone's taste, was a breath of fresh air. Looking at 'crits' of some of the other entertainment on offer in the capital city, I came to the conclusion that the country was 'in danger of sinking beneath the sludge swilling across West End stages and cinema screens.' Once again the letters page started to fill up; it was clear that not everyone liked my blunt denunciations, but some did.

Not content with that little outburst I went along to a performance of the film 'Grease' and expressed surprise that so many parents were sitting in the cinema accompanied by their eight and nine year old daughters and sons. 'What's wrong with that?' many asked then and would probably ask today. But at the time when I was bringing up my own family, I questioned whether a film in which a girl was raped in the back of a car was suitable for children of that age. In today's climate to write articles along these lines would, sad as I am to say it, produce howls of laughter and derision.

With the year 1980 fast approaching and realising that I still had many years to complete before picking up a small pension, I started to plan my escape from Cambridge. I loved the city and still do but it was painful to stay around and watch the decline of an erstwhile excellent regional newspaper. In all fairness it wasn't the only area of Britain where the previously loved 'local rag' was becoming an irrelevance, packed with material that came free through many other channels. The villain of the piece was the free sheet, a bundle of advertisements stitched together to look like a newspaper and dropped through the letter boxes of every accessible household in the city.

The tradition in journalism had always been to learn on the job and it had taken a long time to develop a national training scheme. It was a scheme not given much of a chance because editors did not have the financial freedom to employ young men and women and then send them away to be trained; so even the essential subjects such as government and law were demoted to an evening class. And, as many young people learned to their disadvantage, it wasn't possible to become efficient shorthand writers in a hurry. Typing was generally of the two finger variety.

18

Training Wannabe Journalists

In his new role as managing editor of Westminster Press, Nicholas Herbert could see how badly equipped for the job were many of the youngster used as cheap labour in some local newspapers. So he decided he would set up his own training school where promising youngsters could be given the opportunity to concentrate on handling the tools they needed to become efficient reporters.

To my very pleasant surprise, I was invited to be one of the first tutors and this meant a move to St Leonards on Sea on the south coast where a floor of a building on the sea front was equipped to teach juniors from Westminster Press' widespread local newspaper chain. The plan was to have five-month courses during which time much essential information would have to be absorbed as well as learning the correct way to put a balanced story together. One of my tutorial tasks was to teach central and local government which was a gamble of the highest order. My local government knowledge was good but, apart from what I had picked up along the way, I had a very flimsy understanding of the workings of central government. Some of the students who came to us had degrees in politics and social sciences but were very kind to me when they realised I was barely a step ahead of them in understanding the workings of various government departments. During the early courses my ploy was to find a graduate who had studied the ins and outs of nationalisation or the economy and invite him or her to the front of the class to give fellow students the benefit of their superior knowledge. They forgave me, I believe, because they knew in other areas I was advancing their future careers, especially when it came to practical journalism. I must have made progress myself because I was invited to join the National Council for the Training of Journalists and later when made redundant was able to pick up a small, very small fee, marking central and local government examination papers.

The first in-take at this unusual seat of learning was a disaster. Editors had not taken enough care in their choice of youngsters who had the potential to become good reporters and it became obvious that a group of them had chosen journalism because they couldn't think of anything else to do. One lad was so bored with the whole procedure that he had a habit of turning his back on the tutor and dragging his feet down one of the walls. Despite this behaviour, there was something about this lad which made me think he might make the grade. The only time he showed an interest was when we started to dissect the technique of gathering and presenting a story. I was rewarded two years later when I had a letter out of the blue saying that he was making great strides on a good regional newspaper.....and he was enjoying himself. He concluded with a thank you.

Some of the degree students who came on later courses said it was much harder work than listening to lectures at university and nearly all of them struggled to acquire the 100 words-a-minute shorthand certificate they needed if their editors were going to take them on permanently. I knew what they were going through but my sympathies were muted; I had been forced into using a smattering of Pitman's outlines three weeks into my first job whereas they were being given five months to master the skill.

More enjoyable was my role of introducing them to the task of digging deep for stories and this meant leaving the classroom when the lifeboat flares went up and heading for the beach to find out what was happening. We also went as a group to courts, inquests, inquiries and council meetings and on occasions picked up stories local employed reporters had missed.

One of the most hilarious occasions was when the whole 'class' turned up at a parish council meeting in the quiet coastal village of Fairlight. The councillors had never seen one reporter let alone 15 and were completely thrown by the thought that what they were saying could actually be reported. To begin with they tried to argue that only people living in the parish could attend but in a very good natured way later accepted that coming under such scrutiny was good for them as well as the young people listening. The clerk confided that he had never known the quality of debates improve so noticeably in all the time he had worked in the parish. I always stayed with the students so that I could monitor their copy and also point out where they had completely failed to see the prospect of following up a story outside the council chamber. Another advantage of being with them was that if there was a promising debate, I could take the best report to one of the local papers scattered along the south coast. They were happy to print the story if they knew I had been supervising the output. Before long we had one wall of the school covered with stories produced by the students. An element of competition was introduced because they all wanted to see their story printed and displayed on the 'classroom' notice board.

On one occasion when we disrupted shorthand lessons to investigate why the Hastings lifeboat had been called out, I cast doubt on their keenness when they arrived back after a 15 minute absence agreeing that it was a waste of time 'there was nothing worth reporting.' While they buried their heads in their shorthand notebooks again I wandered across to the beach in time to greet the lifeboat crew pulling a small motorboat to the shore. After listening to what the skipper told me I invited him to visit the training centre the next day to tell the students what he had told me. Faces started to go red and heads were hung low as the friendly skipper explained that a small boat, its outboard motor useless, had drifted into the middle of the most dangerous part of the English Channel and the occupants had been in danger of being mowed down by one of the gigantic vessels steaming through this overcrowded strip of water. The lesson they learned was not to accept the first and probably uninformed explanation but to stick around and keep probing.

When a new batch of students arrived I usually sent them out onto the prom to hear first hand what visitors to the seaside town thought about Hastings and St Leonards. The instruction was not to move more than a couple of hundred yards in either direction from the front door of the training centre. This enabled me to watch them at work from my office window and although I couldn't hear their questions or the answers it was possible to assess who combined boldness with a polite approach when trying to obtain opinions from members of the public. One attractive but painfully shy student recoiled noticeably when a busy pedestrian told her he was not interested in her survey and pushed her out of the way. I recall she had a string of beads which snapped and she spent the rest of the allotted time picking up the beads one by one. Her questionnaire contained very little information of any merit and one had to come to the conclusion that she was probably not going to make it as a reporter who could face up to all sorts of responses from the people she went to interview.

There were some extraordinary incidents, too. One day the centre seemed to be ominously empty during and after the lunch break and for a while I discussed with the other tutors whether they thought we had worked them so hard, they had gone on strike. We learned sometime later that two of the students had slipped off to the registrar's office....to get married. The bride had already been a problem in other ways, once fooling around with her husband-to-be and managing to fall on her back and head when attempting to relieve her boredom with a dangerous gymnastic routine. She was kept in hospital overnight and I found myself in the role of her messenger boy, letting her parents and others know that there was nothing seriously wrong. That was a long night but there was another early-hours episode when a phone call informed me that one of the girl students was in a terrible state and threatening all sorts of things because she felt she was doing so badly on the course. I had to do something but there was a little voice in the back of my head which said be careful about going into the room of a girl student late at night. I had every reason to be careful because the welcome I got was, to say the least of it, rather on the friendly side. I gave her a few words of advice and encouragement from the doorway and beat a hasty retreat. The girl went on to do quite well and we remained good friends....from a distance! It was not all hard work. As Christmas approached we went as a group to France on the Newhaven ferry. The task was to compare prices with goods on the English south coast and try to come to a conclusion whether a trip across the channel saved money or left the day-tripper out of pocket. We came to the conclusion that not many crossed the channel with the purpose of saving money; more attention was given to acquiring a supply of good French wine and delicious cheese for the Christmas festivities.

19

Disturbing the Peace in Bexhill

One of the joys of this pioneer job was that there were reasonably long breaks between courses and I was again able to indulge myself in my favourite hobby, singing light opera. My first group in Cambridge was nicknamed SLOG for short; my new group along the coast at Bexhill on Sea was known as BLODs. After a couple of shows singing in the chorus an unexpected opportunity arose when a dispute broke out between one of the well-known amateur south coast performers and the producer. He had a powerful music hall style voice and had been chosen to play Grieg in 'The Song of Norway'. After he had gone off in a huff, the producer very reluctantly decided I was her only prospect if the show was to go ahead. Being a light tenor, I had a difficult job trying to penetrate the vast expanse of the De La Warr pavilion at Bexhill, which is large enough to cater for conferences, trade fairs and boxing bouts. There were several former D'Oyly Carte performers in the seaside town, and an unusually high proportion of senior citizens. Some of the former 'pros' joined the BLODS chorus and it was a real pleasure to be one of a group of men who sang their harmonies with precision and pleasure. Taking on my first major role in such company was a different matter altogether and a challenge indeed.

When I did steal a glance into the auditorium I was aware of a sea of purple rinses and I had been warned it was an audience which expected a high standard from its local light opera group. The real star of the show was the highly talented pianist who played an extract from the Grieg piano concerto at the end of the show but I had to give the impression I was the virtuoso, using a stage piano made of extremely fragile material. I did play the piano at a low grade level and was at least able to strike the fake keys in convincing manner. Each evening the sweat would pour from my face and as my enthusiasm got the better of me another piece of the wood or cardboard from which the piano was made would fall onto the stage floor. From an acting point of view I believe I made a reasonable stab at the part but the nightly battle was trying to get my voice to reach beyond the first three rows of the stalls. My wife, Susan, who was doing front of house duties delighted in telling the story of two elderly women members of the audience who walked through the foyer at the end of the show discussing why it was necessary to have a woman in the orchestra pit sitting in front of a piano when the chap playing Grieg on stage was doing such a good job. That certainly was a pat on the back as far as my acting was concerned but their reaction to my singing was not recorded.

Back in the training centre, the second course and the ones that followed were, thankfully, quite different from our catastrophic first efforts. Editors had got the message about choosing their candidates wisely and most of them started an early search for youngsters with an appetite for journalism. That meant identifying a number of essential qualities like an ability to put a sentence together, an insatiable curiosity, determination and plenty of reserves of energy. It was our job to teach the techniques of interviewing, constructing a story, essential elements of law and government and to instil in the students the need to present balanced stories and not reports that were heavily laced with their own opinions. Sadly, that requirement has been cast aside by many of today's tabloids and it is often difficult to differentiate between news and comment. One student sent out to cover a local election turned in a piece of copy that demonstrated his disgust with the result. 'Don't do that again,' he was told, 'or you'll be looking for another job.' Most upsetting for me was the number of young journalists who, when they returned to their newspapers. found that the passion we had tried to generate evaporated when they were tied to a desk and a telephone and rarely had a chance to spread their wings in the big world outside the office.

In so many ways my days at St Leonards on Sea were some of the happiest and most challenging of my journalistic career. They were spoiled only by the feeling that because of the turmoil in the newspaper industry during the 80s we were wasting our time. Some of our youngsters went on to make a name for themselves on national newspapers but almost as many called me to say: 'It was all very well you trying to infect us with your enthusiasm for the job but all we do is fill in the gaps between the advertisements with anything that happens to be on hand.'

I would probably have been wise to stay at the seaside and enjoy an assortment of activities between courses---singing, fishing, tennis as well as a good social life---but I failed to rid myself of the misguided ambition to edit my own newspaper. There were plenty of opportunities within the Westminster Press empire and I tried to persuade the managing directors of various regional newspapers that I was the man to lead their editorial teams. I came under consideration for top jobs at Bradford, Doncaster and Bath but the powers-that-be decided that someone who had been out of the heat of the kitchen for almost five years would probably find it difficult to cope, not only with putting together a daily newspaper but also dealing with some of the problems associated with new technology and the growing bitterness of printers who saw themselves as victims of progress.

In the end I got my editor's job but it was not what I had in mind. The chair I was offered and eventually took was at the Biggleswade Chronicle, a small but much respected newspaper of record under the umbrella of Bedford County Press. Having just enjoyed some happy years meeting the challenge of developing young talent, I was now about to embark on two of the most miserable years of my life. What I didn't know when I accepted the job was that the managing director in Bedford, Colin Houghton, was already planning mass slaughter of his editorial staff right across the group. Our first meeting was barely credible. A couple of week previously I had called into the little Biggleswade office and met a staff of a chief sub-editor, a sports editor and four reporters. The managing director offered no greeting, no words of encouragement, no suggestions of how he would like to see the Biggleswade Chronicle brought into the 21st century. An anachronism, it certainly was, but much loved by the townspeople and those who lived in country villages around. His first words were: 'You'll have to get rid of two of your reporters now and probably another one very soon.' There was no plan at this stage about how the pages of the newspaper would be filled without reporters and no apology for moving me and my family 80 miles north to act as executioner. I was being asked to wield the axe without any knowledge of the roles and abilities of staff under me. It was an appalling situation but looking back I think I received some divine help because two of the younger members of the staff, who probably knew more about what was coming than I did, offered themselves up as a sacrifice. They had already done their research, sensed what was about to happen and had lined up new jobs.

Personally, I found that in no way reassuring and received a further blow when the very dedicated chief sub-editor, Sue Steptoe, decided she would have a better future doing public relations work for the Royal Society for the Protection of Birds. The sub-editing side of the work was not my strength but I now found myself faced with umpteen pages to fill, plus a huge editing and lay-out task. Just at the point when I felt matters couldn't get worse, the sports editor decided he had had enough. This was a tremendous loss because he was the only person who knew how to decipher the scores of reports that came from clubs all around the county. A particular difficulty was that he had always been prepared to accept reports of matches, tournaments and league tables on any sort of material that had a small area of white space…and this included the backs of cigarette packets and used envelopes. For the amateur scribes in Biggleswade new technology was a long way off.

There had been many rough periods and plenty of intensive work when I was working in Bath as a young man, but my first year with the tiny Biggleswade Chronicle was purgatory. With limited skills in designing, one page could take me an hour, twenty or thirty pages were quite beyond me. At this stage I had a couple of juniors (later reduced to one) to gather the news, the rest I had to do myself. Once a week I had to face an encounter with disgruntled printers in Bedford, and they managed to reduce me to a jibbering wreck, which was part of their disruption strategy. Having left my wife and sons in St Leonards while our house was still on the market, I stayed with an old Cambridge News friend, Ivor Harvey, who lived in a village close to the A1. He was one of the most capable sub-editors in the game and with great skill and patience guided me towards producing my first pages for Biggleswade readers. I don't think they were impressed with my contribution because they had all come to venerate Fred Simms, an editor of long standing, and didn't like the fact that Westminster Press had allowed him to retire.

I calculated it would take ten years at least to be recognised by the public I was serving but I wasn't going to be allowed one complete year let alone ten. While I was doing the best I could, even to the point of researching and writing one piece of investigative journalism, secret negotiations were going on to sell all the Bedford papers to EMAP. When this happened it was not long before a decision was made to get rid of all the editorial staff in places like Biggleswade and produce the paper from Bedford. So my dream of editing my own newspaper evaporated before I could savour even a modicum of power, not that it was power I was seeking. All I wanted to do was to produce a lively local newspaper and go home at night thinking it had reflected the lives of the people around me, as well as making sure local bureaucrats and dishonest traders were not having it all their own way. Within a year the entire operation was taken out of my hands for purely economic reasons and for several months while working out my redundancy I was reduced to walking along the town's river bank thinking about what might have been. I don't think the retailers, the councillors, the sportsmen in the area or the ordinary citizens even noticed I had been among them. When we did meet up they usually asked: 'Where's Fred Simms? He usually comes to our events.'

Finding another job in the battered and shattered newspaper industry (many other regional organisations were going through the same troublesome times) was not going to be easy, if not impossible. So from my

Cambridgeshire home I started to scrutinise every piece of printed material to find odd jobs that would keep the wolf from the door. I took my dole money and eked out my savings but resources dwindled fast. Many times I had claimed that if I was ever out of a job I could always find something to keep me and the family going. Now was the time to prove it. Restocking supermarket shelves or returning shopping trolleys to their rightful place was on my 'possibles' agenda but there were more interesting part-time jobs around and because of my amateur stage background I rather fancied being an 'extra' in a film being made on the old wartime airfield at Duxford. The film makers paid £50 for a day's 'work' and handed out whole tins of salmon for lunch. The work amounted to sitting around just in case someone was needed to be a 'passenger' on the disused aircraft they were using in the film. As far as I can remember no one was called on set. Before I headed for home £50 richer, I inquired when the film was likely to go on circuit. The answer was 'probably never'.... only a small number of the films they made ever saw the light of day.

Another of the casual jobs I took on in 1986 was almost as pointless but paid a reasonable daily rate. This was working for the medical newspaper PULSE and involved a journey from Cambridge to Dartford. The news editor insisted I arrived at 9.30am which meant a nasty drive through the rush hour. My brief was to ring various people in the medical world, mainly doctors, and seek their views on all manner of medical problems. During the first week I discovered doctors were never available to talk to journalists, even medical ones, until they had dealt with the usual rush of morning patients. It was also usual practice in those days to go out on visits once their surgeries had been emptied so I cannot remember ever speaking to a doctor until late in the afternoon. I could have set out for home on most days without producing a line of copy but my conscience and old fashioned values wouldn't allow me to do that. I usually stayed in the hope of tracking down the doctor I wanted before he went home for supper.

My third 'temp' job seemed just up my street because it involved taking media classes at Luton College of Higher Education. All that experience at St Leonards on Sea would now come in useful as I embarked on another attempt to help keen, young would-be reporters. Young they might have been but keen they certainly were not. Over a number of weeks at the college I came across only two students who were really hungry for a job in newspapers. Most of them had chosen media studies because it seemed an easy option and would avoid the necessity of doing any work for a couple of years. To my dismay their behaviour was on a par with the disastrous first intake at St Leonards. I tried to persuade them that to succeed in any branch of the media they would have to learn the basics and the basics could best be learned on a well edited, small weekly newspaper. Getting that across was rather like trying to float a 10-ton piece of lead on the River Ouse. One girl said she wanted to apply for jobs on fashion magazines and could I gear my teaching to the best way to fulfil this ambition. One of the boys, who had hardly said a word for the first hour of the first session, suddenly looked up and said he might as well go and join a different course because he wanted to be a film director. What possible use would it be to him to know how to write up local weddings and obituaries. Luton College later obtained university status but I have never been back to see if it developed a genuine media course. My impression while there was that they were using people like me just to put up a show and fill the time of unenthusiastic youngsters who didn't know or care about what they would do with their lives. What Luton and similar colleges needed to realise, and still need to realise, is that a media course which tempts young people to think that they can become a sports writer or a fashion editor overnight is wasting everyone's time. While the college was prepared to pay me a respectable fee for doing this job, I stuck at it and was able to guide the only two keen students on the course in a direction that should have given them a good chance of persuading an editor somewhere that they might have the right attitude and instincts to become journalists.

20

Retreat into Public Relations

Rescue from this unsatisfying way of earning a living came when I was offered a job in public relations. An early reaction was to say: 'No, not at any cost.' But Barry Simmons who ran a small but very successful public relations firm in Luton could see how I might be useful, not only with my journalistic experience but also exploiting my knowledge of local government. Barry considered my time as an examination adjudicator for the National Council for the Training of Journalists might carry some weight when attracting non-commercial clients such as local authorities and hospital trusts. I did quite enjoy promoting a new hospital at Dartford and built up a good rapport with councillors at St Neots when they decided they wanted a better public image. But I had to swallow very hard when building companies tried to utilise our skills to put across messages that were deliberately misleading. One of them, when seeking publicity for a new housing estate, gave specific instructions that the route for a new by-pass a few hundred yards away should not be mentioned in a press release. Against all my better instincts I had to find a way around that dilemma, conscious that Barry could lose a valuable client if I didn't appear to toe the line. It was a question of playing with words and my solution was to mention the by-pass but to emphasise the advantages it might have for people living on the estate. The press release, like so many others was never used, the newspapers receiving it preferring to put their own slant on the story. Today the majority of free sheets would not even bother to check the content, so would give companies and other organisations freedom to say what they liked, as long as they advertised, of course.

A more amusing project was endeavouring to put a newsletter together for Bedfordshire County Council. Politically they had a hung 'parliament' so every issue of any importance ended in stalemate. Before putting the newsletter 'to bed' I had to get the agreement of the leaders of all three major parties. Each would offer their views, for example on the council's forthcoming budget proposals, and each had to see each other's contribution. This meant they would put the blue pencil through anything they didn't like and when the proof came back to me the remnants were a dog's dinner and of no help to the people the council was supposed to be serving. If there was an editorial policy it was along the lines of producing a news sheet that looked good but never actually said anything.

Barry was a great character and we did have lots of fun. Lunchtime parties in the local Chinese, ferry trips across the Channel and dealing with impossible briefs like persuading the large Chinese population in Luton that the Halifax building society (as it then was) was giving them their own financial banking house. The logo and the stationery went Chinese and, of course, there had to be a Chinese launch party with dragons and all the trimmings. Much to my surprise Barry offered me a directorship, a nice gesture except that this personal upgrade went exactly the same way as my ill-fated editorship in Bedfordshire. Recession towards the end of the 80s brought financial problems to most small organisations with a cash flow problem and there had to be an amicable break-up between Barry and myself.

I went back to Cambridge and decided to go it alone, acting as a PR and editorial consultant, a one-man affair conducted from my bedroom. 'Fax' machines were just coming into their own and my ancient model, acquired second hand, enabled me to offer speedy press releases to London companies that had been forced to off-load large sections of their own public relations teams. They had retained a few of their inexpensive younger employees who didn't have the first clue how to put a press release together so they would pass their inadequate collection of facts to me whereupon I would speak to their clients, follow any interesting promotion points and then funnel a press release back to them via the facsimile machine. I knew 95 per cent of the content would never be published because it was the sort of material I had spiked daily when running a news desk. But it paid quite well and my accountant son, Adrian, decided I should do all that was necessary to form a viable business. He even helped me draw up a business plan.

***

One sure way of boring people to death is to talk about holidays but there was one out-of-the-ordinary holiday in 1989 that was supposed to celebrate our 30th wedding anniversary. Our planned destination was the island of Antigua but as things turned out we would not even set eyes on its attractions, not under normal conditions anyway. At Heathrow while waiting with Sue's sister, Yvonne, and her husband, Frank, we were warned that over the Atlantic there was a problem---a seasonal hurricane promising to be one of the worst for a very long time. We could cancel if we liked but the pilot would do his best to fly over or around the turbulent area. To this day we're not quite sure why we decided to take the risk but we were anticipating the trip so keenly that common sense went out of the window. We were not in the air for long before the British Airways pilot received a disturbing update and opted to take his passengers to Puerto Rico rather than Antigua. The hurricane decided to change direction, too.

The wind was already strengthening when we touched down and were ushered to the Hotel La Concha, a beach-side hotel where the proprietor had already decided he could make a small fortune by offering rooms to the stranded passengers. This was not going to be appreciated by those who had hotel rooms booked in Antigua and assumed BA would pay for their mistake. The belief that we would be taken to our dream island in the morning was quickly shattered when to our amazement the BA pilot, presumably now aware of the direction in which Hurricane Hugo was heading, decided to make a fast exit. No one was offered a lift to somewhere that might have been a safe haven and so the only thing to do was to enjoy the scenery for a few hours and hope the forecast of 140 mph winds had been exaggerated.

On this occasion, we were to discover the men in the weather stations were spot on but initially the wind was strong, not menacing. We went onto the beach where the palm trees were bending and the waves were beginning to look a touch on the vicious side but this turned out to be just the overture. As the wind strengthened we sought refuge in a small wood structured beach-side café and a bemused manager wondered why we were still hanging around. 'It's not going to be very nice when it arrives' he told us, 'better to get away from the beach area,' he advised. He smiled grimly when we pretended we were tough Brits and could take what was coming. We didn't really appreciate the seriousness of his warning until the next afternoon when, allowed out of the safety of the hotel, we discovered his café no longer existed. It had been blown away along with all the kitchen equipment which might have been used to make our breakfast.

The night spent in the hotel is not one likely to be forgotten by any of the guests. Everyone had beaten a hasty retreat apart from the British Airways passengers. Those who had intended to holiday at the La Concha had headed for safer ground. In answer to our question about how long the hurricane would last (an innocent question which assumed the hurricane had been raging for some time) we were told that Hugo had not yet arrived and when it did it might be accompanied by a sea surge. We all looked at the big picture windows and started to wonder how long they would stand up to a blasting by 140 mph winds and crashing surf. During the next few hours the lighting failed, fresh water stopped running and we were advised to collect blankets from our rooms and head for the basement where portable gas stoves were already alight in an effort to provide warm soup for guests and anyone who came off the streets seeking refuge.

I have several enduring memories, one being the state of the bedroom when we were allowed upstairs the following day. The windows were gone, the carpets and bedclothes soaked, leaving the bathroom the only part of the 'luxury suite' untouched by the fury of the storm. My wife, Sue, disappeared for a while and emerged from the bathroom holding a toothbrush and a bottle of gin. There was no clean water, she said, so she had used the gin to clean her teeth. The public areas of the hotel looked as if they had been struck by a bomb and people were wandering around aimlessly, asking whether British Airways officials were on their way to arrange a quick getaway. That was not going to happen. The airport was strewn with debris and light aircraft blown around like a child's toy. The only planes allowed in and out were those bringing supplies for the islanders, left with nothing after their fragile huts had been ripped to pieces. We should have been out there giving a hand but to our shame stood around complaining about everyone and everything. Some passengers were on their way to a wedding, another couple said they would not now be able to attend the funeral of a much loved relative. When we did eventually head for the airport to wait for a seat on one of the relief planes, I was filled with remorse as I looked out of the coach window and saw the plight of the Puerto Ricans. But we had been told, in answer to suggestions that we might be able to help, that the locals would get on better with what they had to do without having disgruntled Brits hanging about the place.

In a strange way I had enjoyed the episode because I had been able to take my mind off the dangers by doing some real reporting from an area which had become the focus of attention in most parts of the world. I found one telephone line which seemed to be working and was able to feed dramatic coverage back to all branches of the media. I had one huge professional disappointment. Having gone to great lengths to get a descriptive piece back to the Sunday Times at their request, the IRA decided to explode a bomb in the heart of London and all my material was despatched to the spike. Already Hurricane Hugo had become yesterday's news. Back at home I found various newspaper clippings confirming that some of my efforts had been worthwhile but I was ashamed of the piece which claimed I was demanding an apology and compensation from BA. If I did say this it was an unguarded moment, speaking from my devastated bedroom. I should have known better.

We had planned a visit to the States as the second part of our holiday and as the relief plane was going in that direction anyway we decided to find a comfortable hotel and do the things we intended to do when the 'holiday' was first planned. The adrenaline must still have been flowing when we touched down in Miami because on only the second day we decided to take an early evening trip around an alligator swamp in a fragile looking hovercraft. The boatman insisted on trapping a baby alligator and telling us with pride that its mother was a few yards away but he was not afraid. He could speak for himself; we decided that perhaps Hurricane Hugo posed lesser dangers. When we arrived back at our home in Cambridge, eventually, there was a note on the doormat from our son, Nicholas. It said that a postcard would have been quite adequate; we didn't have to go on the radio to tell him and the rest of the family about our 'holiday'. He had been driving to work one morning and had suddenly heard my voice coming out of the car radio speaker.

21

Born Again—The First Signs

The rest of my life (the last third more or less) has been so different from those earlier years that I feel I should back-peddle and start to identify where, why and how the change started to come about. I had spent nearly five years trying to convince young people that even at a very local level it was possible to make a difference if local issues were examined and reported in a responsible manner. In taking a job on the Biggleswade Chronicle colleagues thought I was committing professional suicide because I would never be allowed to put into practice or demonstrate how powerful journalism could benefit society at local as well as national level. But it allowed me to achieve a personal ambition. I could now say I had edited a newspaper, even though my earlier experiences of journalism were far more exciting.

We chose to live in Haslingfield, a village to the south side of Cambridge for a number of reasons. We were leaving our eldest son, Adrian, in Hastings which was not very kind because he never wanted to go there in the first place. But he had achieved all the necessary qualifications to become an accountant and already had his first job in Eastbourne. He was also to meet one of the young female reporters in the St Leonards training centre and has partially forgiven me because the relationship blossomed and in 1988 he married Sara at the church in her home village of Princes Risborough. Nicholas, five years younger than his brother, returned to Cambridge with us and one of the reasons for choosing Haslingfield to live was that he could finish his studies at the 6th form college in Hills Road, Cambridge, one of the finest colleges of its kind in the country. Haslingfield was also on the right side of the city, enabling me to set out on my journey to Biggleswade without having to battle with heavy morning traffic.

Although born in Bath, Susan and I had grown very fond of Cambridge and we both looked forward to reuniting with friends we had made in the early years of our married life. I now considered myself a much more competent stage performer and immediately re-established my links with Sawston Light Opera Group. It is said that one shouldn't return to old hunting grounds and expect everything to be as you remembered it in days gone by and this was certainly the case when trying to re-establish myself in a group that had moved on. Because I had had singing lessons on the south coast and was given one lead role in a major production, I thought auditions would be a formality. I was brought down to size when given the role of Alfred in *'Pink Champagne'* a simpler version of Johann Strauss' *'Die Fledermaus'*. Alfred is a high-range tenor who has to woo Rosalinda in song from outside her bedroom window. On an amateur stage this meant standing behind foam-backed scenery and endeavouring to raise one's voice to a volume that could be heard at the back of the auditorium. It was another disaster and affected me to such an extent it ruined my attempts to play a ridiculously romantic scene immediately afterwards. I sounded more like a nervous schoolboy than a passionate Italian tenor and to make matters worse instead of oozing charm across the breakfast table, I forgot my words. I could have said almost anything and the audience would not have noticed but I foolishly tried to stick to the script, and left the audience in a state of bewilderment. With tail between my legs, I returned to the chorus and never regained the confidence to play another major role.

On the plus side I had renewed my friendship with SLOG's musical director, David Adams, who suggested on a number of occasions that I should spare time to visit King's College Chapel on a Sunday afternoon to hear the choir sing a traditional evensong. Still trying to make some sort of living and working all hours God gave me, it was some time before I took up his invitation. I realise now that this was the beginning of a journey which would take me into new pastures. It wasn't my first experience of the King's College choir but perhaps in those heady days as a features editor I was more concerned with making an impression with a punchy review than sitting back and enjoying the sheer beauty of choral singing in the unique surroundings of a famous chapel. I went back once more and then again…and again. I had been a nominal member of the Church of England during boyhood days but had never paused to think too much about the meaning of the words I was singing or what the minister was trying to tell me from the pulpit. Now I was wondering whether it wasn't just the beauty of the music which was taking hold of me. What I was gradually coming to realise was that the sensitive choral singing was churning up feelings that had more than a hint of the spiritual about them.

The truly meaningful breakthrough, if I can call it that, came on a Good Friday when I queued in the courtyard of King's College Chapel with several hundred locals and tourists. In truth, most of us were there to hear an exquisite performance of Italian composer Allegri's *Miserere* and I was certainly not the only one to marvel at the inspiration this piece is capable of imparting. But it was the telling in dramatic form of Jesus' arrest, trial and crucifixion which convinced me I must start listening, rather than allowing the words of John's Gospel to go in one ear and out of the other. At this stage I think the cynical side of my nature would have taken over again if someone had suggested I was at the beginning of a personal relationship with Jesus Christ. But this was precisely what was happening. It could have taken place in the choir stalls of St Michael's Church, Bath, some 50 years earlier, but it didn't. It was no instant conversion but in many ways was an experience made more secure by the slow, methodical progression towards an understanding that there is a creator and we, and all that is around us, didn't arrive on earth as a result of a 'big bang'.

At about this time, another member of the family, my youngest son, Nick, was going through a difficult passage in his life but initially was not prepared to talk about it. To his mother's surprise and later to mine, he confessed to feelings of disillusionment which he could not satisfactorily explain. He had a good home, he said, good parents, a good job and a girl friend, nothing to complain about on the surface but a feeling that something was missing. My mother had recently died and we had noticed he had been particularly upset when attending her funeral in the Bath crematorium. On our return to Haslingfield his mother suggested he called on the local vicar to see if he could help. Nick disappeared for a couple of hours and was certainly thoughtful when he returned. We did not question him, knowing that he would talk about it in his own time.

He had qualified as a chartered surveyor and was working at the Inns of Court in London but what we didn't know was that he had become a regular member of the congregation at All Souls, the evangelical church in Langham Place, London. I don't think he talked about it much in the early days because he felt he had enough on his hands sorting out his own life before he turned his attention to other members of the family. As he grew more confident, things started to move at quite a pace and there was an invitation to his confirmation which came out of the blue. We had arranged a holiday and were unable to attend but by now Nick was sure enough about his faith to take the first tentative steps towards evangelising his parents. He homed in on his parents' love for music and suggested we attended a Proms Praise concert in the National Festival Theatre.

The evening began disastrously. I had a mysterious attack of Tinnitus and couldn't even tolerate the noise made by a small group of musicians playing in the theatre foyer. Nick and his wife Julia were held up on their journey to the theatre and were late. I was uncomfortable and in a bad mood because of the ear condition. It did not seem to be the moment to settle down to listen to a programme of 'proms praise' music by an enthusiastic bunch of amateurs. Amateurs? All were outstanding instrumentalists in a disciplined orchestra backed by singers, some of whom were already playing professionally or were studying at the Royal College of Music. In the interval I quizzed Nick about where these talented people had come from, how much did they have to pay them, why would they give their time to a semi religious occasion. With a smile, he said the only cost was hiring the venue... all the performers were members of the congregation at All Souls. During the second half of the programme I realised that my tinnitus had vanished.

Assessing that we had been moved by what we had seen and heard, Nick followed up with a suggestion that we joined him for a service at All Souls. And what an experience that was, hardly an empty seat and 'on stage' some of the people we had enjoyed listening to in the Festival Theatre. Now they were leading the congregation in a variety of popular hymns with orchestral accompaniment. Looking around there were people from many countries and I later learned it was a favourite place of worship for staff from several of London's embassies. But without doubt 'the star' was an elderly man, John Stott, who although retired had maintained a strong connection with All Souls as rector emeritus. In 2005 the Times magazine declared him as one of the 100 most influential people in the world. During my youth and early twenties I had been in churches where many sermons were given but probably for the first time I found myself actually listening to this one, really listening. John Stott, who died in 2011, was not a flamboyant preacher but his steady, penetrating presentation carried a powerful message that one could not ignore. Without knowing anything about him, I had recently acquired his book *'Basic Christianity'* which I put in my suitcase when Susan and I went on a short break to the Isle of Wight. On a seat overlooking the sea I read it.....and then started to read it again. Sue, a little worried because of the time I had been away, could see that I was totally preoccupied and didn't ply me with questions. But over the next few days I was able to convey to her that a process had started as a result of recent experiences and reading John Stott's book and I hoped I would be able to give her a better explanation when I had absorbed and analysed the content. It may sound cold to talk about 'a process' but my journalistic training demanded a close inspection of the material before me. There was no question of me ever claiming a Damascus Road type of experience. But what was happening was a thrilling follow-up to the emotions experienced at King's College on Good Friday.

People may ponder over what they have just read and question the change of direction of a middle-aged man who never had the time, or rather never found the time, to consider heady questions focused on the meaning of life. But it happened and everything from this time onwards underlines the fact that I had been reborn, incidentally an expression which made me cringe in the early years of my life.

With his mother now plying me with questions and considering whether she, too, could make an open response to the simple but powerful prayer in *Basic Christianity,* Nick was obviously delighted with what he could see might be happening. But he sensibly advocated caution and at our request started to seek out a church in Cambridge where we might get good teaching and the chance to explore the Gospels and the claims that Jesus Christ really did come down to this earth to save sinners and then returned to Heaven to sit at the right hand of his Father.

Our first visit to the Round Church, Cambridge, was not a totally comfortable and uplifting experience. We were nonplussed by the average age of the congregation, most of them students who had omitted to leave their notebooks behind when they left their colleges that morning. They were all writing furiously throughout the sermon and Sue whispered to me that perhaps we had come to the wrong place. A quick survey did reveal that there were some older members of the congregation and some of them, too, were taking notes on the back of their service sheets. The focus for all of them was, of course, the words of the man in the pulpit, the Revd Mark Ashton, who was to play an important part in our Christian journey and in our future lives generally. Mark, who also died in 2011 still in his sixties, was so different from John Stott in a number of ways---he had a commanding voice, delivered his messages with huge strength but out of the pulpit was, in his own words, just another member of his church family. Despite his modesty, we saw him as a great leader and Sue would often say that if he hadn't entered the church might well have been the managing director of a large company. But once he had become a Christian during his college days, Mark could see only one road ahead and that was to work in the service of God.

He took quite a chance with both my wife and I. Sue had not been confirmed when she was a young woman and her request to meet the Bishop at a planned confirmation service might well have been turned down because she had not attended the preparation classes. Mark obviously identified a determination not to wait for a service at some unspecified time in the future and took her under his wing on a one-to-one basis. She was asked to provide proof of her baptism and caused consternation in the office of a high church in Bath when she went in search of her baptism credentials. They were discovered and the confirmation went ahead.

22

Keeping Sunday Special

Mark had a huge influence on the rest of my working life. It was to him I turned when I saw an advertisement in my old newspaper, the Cambridge Evening News, for someone capable of attracting financial support from the country's retailers to support a campaign I had barely heard of *'The Keep Sunday Special Campaign.'* But I thought the experience I had gained in public relations as well as journalism would together give me enough savvy to convince people in all walks of life that a day of rest was worth fighting for. The campaign had its base in the headquarters of the Jubilee Centre, Cambridge, an organisation that based all its research work on Christian ethics. I managed the initial interview well enough but before being offered the job I had to get the minister of my church to confirm that I was a practising Christian. I had been attending the Round Church for only a few months so it was with some trepidation that I approached Mark Ashton and asked him for what amounted to a reference. He looked at me in a manner which suggested he was trying to remember who I was, then smiled and said: 'I don't know a lot about you, John, but I feel I am talking to someone who has very good reasons for wanting to do this job.' So Mark, who didn't make decisions lightly and certainly not under pressure, saw something in me (and subsequently my wife) which convinced him he was not doing the wrong thing. Of course, at that early stage of our Christian lives it probably didn't occur to us that Mark's deep faith had given him the signals he wanted before embracing two people who had spent 50 years claiming Church of England status without undertaking any sort of analysis of what it really meant. As far as my family was concerned developments were taking place at a fast pace. Nick, probably expecting his parents to be a little more than apprehensive, announced that he was giving up his job as a surveyor and was applying for a place at Oakhill Theological College. He had a wife and three children to support and despite our newfound faith we certainly had to bite our bottom lip and refrain from asking; 'However are you going to manage financially?' All I can say after several years is that it worked out well and convinced me that if God is behind your plans you don't need to worry. You probably do worry but it's a wonderful feeling when you realise that this was needless.

Not having to stay around so much to look after a family, the travelling bug took hold and we set out to see a bit more of the world. Again accompanied by Sue's sister Yvonne and her husband Frank, who was able to whistle up time-share accommodation in some of the most unlikely places, we flew into San Francisco spent a while as conventional tourists and then set off in a hired car across country to Sacramento and on to Lake Tahoe. Our friends back at home watched their television sets nervously because by this time we had built up a reputation for drama-packed holidays. As both Los Angeles and San Francisco were on our planned route, some thought it was just a matter of time before an earthquake opened up in front of us! I had a few doubts myself when we were given an elevated room in a 32-storey hotel in the heart of LA. This time we were let off the hook and the only drama while in America was domestic, the news that Henry, our first grandson, had been born. We were able to send a telegram of congratulations from Squaw Valley which somehow seemed appropriate. There was still time for something to happen and failing to recall the perils we had faced on an alligator swamp we set out on another hazardous trip, this time over the Grand Canyon in a tiny plane that was withdrawn from service a very short while after we had been its passengers. The conditions were barely suitable for flying and despite the beautiful scenery below Yvonne spent the entire flight with a newspaper over her head. As the aircraft dipped and dived in the upward and downward flows of air we all had to admit later that we were not as brave as we pretended to be. The trip back to Las Vegas was more comfortable and we were able to look out of the windows and appreciate such sights as the Hoover Dam.

On getting back to the United Kingdom in one piece I was able to plunge into my new job working with a committed group of people at the Jubilee Centre. It was strange at first because we met early each day for a short service of prayers and a hymn. Still not quite sure what was happening to me, I was inclined to look out of the window to see if pedestrians were stopped in their tracks on hearing people singing hymns in such an unlikely corner of the city and on a Monday morning. It was also a regular practice to put aside one day a month as a prayer day and when life got busy there was always the temptation to claim other priorities. The Director of the Centre, Dr Michael Schluter, would have none of it. Prayer came first, he said, or what we were planning to do would have no foundation.

We did raise money from people and organisations still wanting to keep Sunday as a special day and were prepared to open their wallets. Michael Schluter, initially intent on projects demonstrating that the Old Testament contained much information and guidance on almost any subject you could think of, was persuaded after much prayer that the day of rest issue had to be tackled first. Campaigning had not been on his agenda but now he cleared space at the back of his garage and set up a communications base with tentacles stretching out into every corner of the UK. Tens of thousands of pounds were poured into a counter campaign by big stores wanting to increase their profits at any price. Little thought was given to those who would have no option but to leave their families on a Sunday and go to work. The huge efforts make by the KSS team from 1983 until 1994 have been well documented but unpublished was one of my contributions, a document I entitled '*A Slippery Slope*' which charted the huge problems the country faced from the day Parliament decided the big shops could open for six hours. I was in Parliament on that fateful day and listened to some excellent arguments on why the country should at least maintain the status quo. For a couple of optimistic hours we thought we had won the day but at 9.30pm the Commons was flooded with MPs, many still in their dinner jackets, who hadn't listened to one word of the preceding debate but returned merely to cast their vote. That night the Sunday Trading Act received Parliament's blessing and it is not an exaggeration to say from that moment life in Britain started to change radically.

My purpose in writing '*The Slippery Slope*' was not to repeat all the arguments for and against Sunday trading but to record all the unheeded warnings by respected members of the community who claimed the dismantling of the weekend would eventually destroy the strands holding society together. One of the most memorable developments was when the Government majority plummeted to a mere eight votes after a dramatic, emotional speech in the House of Lords by the Earl of Stockton (former Prime Minister, Harold Macmillan). Intervening as the Bill went through the report stage, the former PM told the House of Lords he did not like its contents at all.

He spoke of it being another move 'in the gradual secularisation of our people and against the principles, which made our forebears great'. **He asked the House to remember that the great commandment handed down to God's chosen people was one of the most important pieces of social reform in the history of civilisation---the concept that every man and woman, however humble, should have at least some time to rest.'**

Journalist and broadcaster, John Humphrys, was one of many who joined the debate: **'Here we are free of the drudgery that enslaved us through history, but seemingly determined not to take the opportunity of controlling our own destinies. We have allowed our time---the only irreplaceable commodity each of us owns---to be stolen from us. The weekends have gone. It might have been silly to close the shops on Sunday when we had a day off, but look what has happened now. Half of all working men and a third of women work some or most Sundays.'**

The much respected late David Sheppard, Bishop of Liverpool and an England cricketer, contributed a measured response to the debate: **'As Christians we have no right to impose our values on the whole of society: we have to admit that sometimes in past years the Church has done this. But Christians have the same right to argue for the best view of society that we believe in as other citizens---no more and no less. I believe that society is better off if one day of the week is kept as far as possible, as a different day.'**

The Chief Rabbi, Dr Jonathan Sacks, a man I came to admire very much, had no doubts about the damage the new legislation could cause to family life: **'The** family is where we acquire the skills and language of relationships. It is where we first take the risk of giving and receiving love. It is where one generation passes its values to the next and ensures the continuity of civilisation. For any society, the family is the crucible of its future.'

Some of the more responsible national newspapers echoed these views in various ways. *The Times* forecast that **a selfish and cynical era was just beginning.** *The Guardian* spoke of the nation being **a nation of workaholics** and the *Daily Telegraph* pointed out that **family life was being sacrificed in pursuit of wealth**

My personal contribution to the debate did not set out to say that all the ills of the country could be attributed to the death of Sunday but even a cursory glance at what has happened since demonstrates that many of the problems we now face dated from 1994, the year that Sunday trading became widespread. It signalled, but did not necessarily cause, all sorts of unfortunate developments---closure of post offices and village shops, the isolation of the elderly and handicapped in villages with poor transport, the collapse of small and medium size firms, binge drinking encouraged by round-the-clock availability of alcohol and growing concern about family breakdown as more and more parents went to work at weekends. If ever there was a time when society needed a new broom and when people needed to re-examine their priorities then this had to be it.

23

Parliament under a Banyan Tree

What was needed at this time was a period when we could take a long hard look at our quality of life, or lack of it, and reflect on people's lifestyles in other parts of the world. My scrapbook gives pride of place to an account of a group of tribesmen from a Pacific Island who visited the UK seeking enlightenment. Their chief, Chief Yata, who was accustomed to conducting his 'parliament' cross-legged under a banyan tree, perplexed his people when he returned home and recounted tales of a people who lived in parts of the world they hitherto had considered civilised. The Chief and four of his tribe's people were horrified to come across people in Britain lying in the streets in dirty rags, sleeping under cardboard and begging for money from passers-by. And yet, said the puzzled natives, there are places where dogs are shampooed, powdered and had their hair cut. Why weren't the homeless people given one of the many empty houses that were everywhere? Where were the families of these poor people? they asked. In their 'backward' island, food was shared with those who were less fortunate and anyone finding himself without a home had a hut built for him by the entire village. Everything in his island home, Chief Yata pointed out, revolved around the family, the underlying theme being love and respect. Not so in the British Isles.

The passing of the 1994 Sunday Trading Act was a bitter blow to Michael Schluter and he stepped back from the campaign and went about other tasks he had previously postponed. Funding understandably dropped away and the initial verdict of the team was that the battle had probably been lost. Although I expected to get my marching orders at this point, I did find other useful work to do in the Jubilee Centre and decided to stay around for a while. It was just as well because I was one of the few people in the centre who understood the issues of the Keep Sunday Special campaign and had followed its journey through to the Commons debate. For some time I sat in the corner of a room doing other jobs but getting more and more frustrated by the number of calls still coming from newspaper, radio and television reporters. The big stores, by no means satisfied with the six hours of Sunday trading they had been granted, started to devise little schemes to get around the law. The popular media, mostly against the campaign to save Sunday when it was in full swing, now did one of its notorious U-turns and decided almost en masse to challenge the big companies who were breaking the law. What was the Keep Sunday Special Campaign doing about it? They kept asking so I grabbed the phone and for a while acted as public relations officer. Frustrating as it may have been to have all this attention when a few months earlier it had been sometimes impossible to get our arguments across, I took the initiative and started to state the case for shop workers, small retailers and those in more remote communities who were suffering from the closure of village shops because they could not compete with the superstores. Television appearances and radio interviews became the norm and I had to make quick adjustments to fill the role of interviewee rather than reporter. It was quite stimulating. Suddenly people were stopping me in the street and saying 'saw you on the tele last night.'

I had to suffer one horror interview when, without doing any research on the programme, I finished up talking on a late night radio programme which reached the depths of bad taste. The interviewer (I've forgotten his name now but those in the know still ask me how I managed to get involved with him) seemed intent on making me admit that I was trying to tell everyone how they should lead their lives. There was no way of dodging a series of questions which were carefully designed to embarrass me. I thought I was quite tough until I came up against this particular Rottweiler.

Television producers took first prize for wasting money on a grand scale. An entire outside broadcasting team turned up outside my house one day armed with all the paraphernalia they might have used at a Christmas carol service in King's College Chapel (much to the bewilderment of neighbours who must have thought I had done something terrible). They went away with 15 minutes of detailed discussion and comment but used one sound-bite of their choice lasting 10 seconds. A similar waste of resources was in evidence when I was invited to appear on the BBC's Sunday morning *'Heaven and Earth'* show. They wanted me in Manchester but failed to send the promised taxi at the appointed time. Another car was ordered and I was rushed to a hotel with no time for food, just a few hours to lay down my head. I had been asked to deal with a particular aspect of the campaign but the chosen topic was never raised and I finished up making one comment that did nothing to inform the listener of anything remotely helpful to the campaign. There were others on the show who received similar treatment. The whole exercise probably cost the licence payers several hundred pounds. No wonder people get annoyed when they see how their annual licence fee is spent.

For many years the supermarkets did all in their power to nullify the law which enforced the six-hours-only rule on a Sunday. Initially, they were asking for the permitted shopping period to be increased to nine. Then there was a change of mood brought about by more difficult trading conditions. A public opinion poll suggested that most shoppers would be content to stick to six hours so long as their local corner shop remained open for a few of the essentials. Even Tesco was having second thoughts. A survey arranged by them revealed very few of their customers were in favour of full deregulation. Tesco's change of heart was a blow to concerns like Asda, Ikea, Kingfisher, Next and B&Q. It was probably at this stage that the Government decided another battle over Sunday trading was not in its best interests. The Association of Convenience Stores had been making its presence felt, warning that longer hours for the supermarkets on a Sunday would force even more small traders to close.

A lull in the campaign allowed Sue and I to embark on a journey which we felt would give some depth and vigour to our new found faith. Peter Marshall and his wife Selina, had moved with us from the famous, but tiny Round Church in the centre of Cambridge to a much larger church building due to be demolished and turned into a supermarket. There had been an amazing response to an appeal and St Andrew the Great, destined to be pulled down and converted into another monument to consumerism, became a living church again and was able to extend its ministry to hundreds more Cambridge University students as they passed through the city year after year. Peter had an ambition to take a party from STAG (an abbreviation that quickly became familiar to everyone) on a pilgrimage to the Holy Land and he started to make his plans many months before our departure date. These plans included well prepared talks by Peter designed to put us in the picture before we became absorbed in the historic Jerusalem and other places which he knew would bring the Bible to life.

All who have spent time in Israel will be aware that many pages could be written about a trip like this but I will choose our visit to the Mount of Olives and the gardens of Gethsemane as the two highlights which particularly moved me. Just to sit there, imagining Jesus and his disciples moving across the landscape filled me with wonder. Peter was asked whether we thought Jesus knew the crowds hailing him with Hosannas on one day would be shouting 'crucify him' in such a very short time. Did he know that this triumphant journey into Jerusalem was to end on the cross? 'We can be quite certain that he did know what was going to happen,' said Peter with true conviction. Then he asked us to turn to that part of our Bibles where he had broken this news to his disciples. By the time we had walked The Via Dolorosa (The way of the cross) we, too, shared that conviction. We all wanted to pray and that was what we did.

In spite of my half promise not to bombard the reader with long accounts of holidays, as a new Christian I have to mention the joys of a trip to Oberammergau in 2000 for the passion play which is staged by the villagers every ten years. Apart from it all happening in a beautiful part of the world, the staging of the play was breathtaking. Although the audience is under cover the stage is partly in the open air allowing the natural background to be utilised instead of fabricated scenery. The locals expect the natural elements to play a part in the performance but I was more than a little surprised when a sudden rush of wind moved the trees at the precise time Jesus was being unceremoniously lifted onto the cross. If we hadn't 'spotted' Judas and one or two other characters attending to their cottage vegetable patches in the morning, sporting splendid beards and very old fashioned hair styles, perhaps it wouldn't have penetrated the brain that the cast on the stage were all amateurs, albeit talented amateurs who had been rehearsing for a very long time. Timing was such that the children needed for various parts of Christ's story were able to attend their lessons for part of the day and make their appearances as and when they were wanted. I rashly promised to take my children and grandchildren to the 2010 performance but was not able to meet that commitment. God willing perhaps I will be able to pack a wheel chair and make it in 2020.

The campaign to retain remnants of Sunday never ceased and **July 6, 2006** turned out to be something of a red-letter day for KSS when the Trade Secretary of that time, Alistair Darling, said a consultation exercise had revealed '**no substantial demand for change.**' The time seemed to be ripe for a fresh appraisal of how society should be organised with the interests of the family at the top of the agenda. The time also seemed to be ripe for me, now in my 70th year, to step aside and allow a new, young team to take up the cudgels.

24

St Peter in the Pub

Nick, after ordination, had moved to Lincoln as a curate in a city centre church a stone's throw from Lincoln cathedral. In time he was made an associate vicar and embraced an experiment within the Church of England labelled 'fresh expressions' which acknowledged that fewer people were stepping over the threshold of a church so the church had to go out and meet the people. Where better than in a public house in the middle of a large housing estate? St Peter in the Pub was born and in the early days a service was held one Sunday a month with an in-built facility for young children. People on the Carlton Estate were attracted by the informal nature of the service and to Nick's delight he was able to take over the spacious lounge bar for another two Sundays. The pub became a hive of activity on a Sunday morning as coffee and croissants were served and special arrangements made to keep the children happy. Nick's wife Julia became a key helper in the operation and what was apparent to residents and visitors alike was the special place the couple held in the hearts of many living in an area of Lincoln where church-going was not a regular practice. Their initiative was given a big boost at the start of 2014 when the Archbishop of Canterbury, the Most Rev Justin Welby, released the results of an 18-month study demonstrating that informal congregations (those meeting in pubs and schools etc) had boosted C of E membership by thousands--- the equivalent of an entire diocese. St Peter in the Pub set up at the Lincolnshire Poacher was especially mentioned in a Daily Telegraph report as an example of unusual venues which across the country had drawn 21,000 people.

My other son, Adrian, an accountant on the south coast, frequently found he had an out-of-hours duty helping his wife, Sara, provide a haven for the youth of Newhaven, some of them from troubled backgrounds. For Sara, it was one of those part-time jobs in the Church of England that quickly evolve into full-time occupations. Some of the children made life difficult for her but she never lost heart.

For Susan and I, life didn't change all that much. The KSS campaign still wanted to draw on my experience from time to time but a new challenge was being part of a church plant from St Andrew the Great in the heart of Cambridge to All Saints, Little Shelford, a small village church six miles from the centre of the city. The 30 or so adults with their families received a generous welcome on the whole but the big task was persuading some long established village residents that we were not a crowd of noisy, flag-waving charismatics. Fortunately the curate at St Andrew the Great (STAG), Christopher Ash, had come with us and such was the inspiration he engendered, it was not long before people from a wide area were homing in on Little Shelford to benefit from his faithful presentation of God's word. This was happening at a time when the media were insisting that church attendance in the UK was fast diminishing; not so in churches where teaching from the Bible and reaching out into the community were right at the top of the priorities.

To my amazement Christopher asked me to give the occasional talk from the pulpit and while I always felt I had no right to be there because of a lack of theological training, it was a tremendous privilege to be entrusted with such a task. I started to enjoy the experience once

I had realised preparation for a sermon was rather like preparation for a newspaper or magazine feature. My technique was to concentrate on research from a number of commentaries, then present a message adopting some of the journalistic techniques I had practised for many years. This development was taken a stage further when I decided to try my hand at a novel with an evangelical tweak. My hope was, and still is, that Christians would hand the book to non-Christian friends who might find themselves examining their attitude to life and deciding whether they believed in a creator God. *'Spoofed and Spiked'* presented the challenge --- 'if you found yourself trapped in a cellar for some time with only the Bible as a companion would you read it?' The book was not an overwhelming success because I could never make up my mind whether I was intent on highlighting a declining newspaper industry or endeavouring to steer the reader towards a more serious study of God's word. In fact, the core of the story about the deviousness of a self-proclaimed teenage psychic had merit (most of it was true) but sadly by mixing genres, I believe I fell between two stools. Some of my friends made it clear that that was what I had done.

But it was a sound learning curve for my second piece of serious writing which traced the life of a man who had run away from school and lived on the streets for most of his teenage life. Miraculously, he overcame his inability to read or write to become, after conversion, a very popular and effective Baptist minister. Mike McDade's initial training for life had been highly unconventional, taking on a job which involved climbing to the top of Blackpool tower and applying a preservative to the metal structure and later creating his own business in the fruit and vegetable market. In between, now feeling brave enough to take on the world, he joined the Army and qualified for a spell of service in the Parachute Regiment. His acceptance as a Baptist minister has helped many to re-adjust their attitude to the possibility of miracles. A former Archbishop of Canterbury, Lord Carey, described Mike as one of Jesus Christ's 21st century disciples. The publishers insisted on a catchy title for the book--- *'Runaway, Red Beret and Reverend'* --- not my choice but I had to admit their intervention on this aspect of the book proved rewarding. The argument is that to sell a book, even a Christian book, it has to have an eye catching title.

***

So how did a greenhorn cub reporter manage to make a go of things in the unpredictable battlefields of journalism and public relations, survive for a while trying to form his own business during a deep recession, switch to working for a Christian research and campaigning organisation, give sermons from the pulpit of a local church and finally write a book which described in dramatic fashion how God takes people from any sort of background and turns them into his disciples? The simple answer I was tempted to give was---I don't know. It just happened.

But that isn't true. Such an answer is an insult to the God who planned my life long before I was in the womb and then helped me to continue life's journey no matter what pitfalls hindered my progress. He gave me free will to go in any direction I chose and knew I would make a mess of things from time to time. But he provided all the evidence I needed to come to the conclusion that there was more to life than a successful career and a house full of worldly possessions. He also taught me that in making my choices there would always be conflict. I now see that one of the reasons why I never 'graduated' from the regional press to the national press was my understanding that Fleet Street, London, held greater dangers than Silver Street, Bristol. That is not to belittle some of the great journalism generated in the city of London but on a personal level I could never see myself enjoying the cut-throat tactics of a typical tabloid. It is one thing to stand on a doorstep in quest of a properly researched story which would right a wrong or put a criminal behind bars; a very different matter if the only excuse for intrusion is to find out who is sleeping with whom. I would have derived much satisfaction from revealing the names of those MPs who were lining their pockets at the expense of the taxpayers but would not have enjoyed being asked to identify the mistresses of an over-paid footballer. Spying on Princess Margaret and her intended, hoping to discover a series of indiscretions, cured me of any desire for that sort of journalism.

I could turn to a number of Christian writers who would help me wind up this personal story with a flash of inspiration but I have chosen an extracts from a book *'Distinctives---daring to be different in an indifferent world'* by Vaughan Roberts, Rector of St Ebbe's Church, Oxford. He tells the story of a friend who trained as a doctor *(everyone approves of that – medicine is a worthy profession).* But when he discovered he was gifted as a Bible teacher, he gave up medicine to train at Bible college. That made no sense to his friends. They were even more bemused when he decided to go to Africa. They would have understood if he had gone to use his medical skills, but in fact he went to teach the Bible. What the friend of Vaughan Roberts saw was a greater need for people to hear about Jesus than to have their bodies healed. So he gave up medicine. The world thought he was mad but his explanation was that he was living for the future, not the present.

I am very grateful to God that this view, unpopular as it may be in the 21st century, has infiltrated to members of my family and to some of my friends. My wish is that many more will at least follow this path of inquiry leading to a future that may be beyond their wildest dreams. Even the most casual analysis of life in Britain today indicates that a huge number of people are convinced they have no future beyond the grave when readily at hand, like an unopened gift under the Christmas tree, is the most wonderful present anyone could imagine.... God's promise of forgiveness and eternal life, explained simply but powerfully in the gospels of the New Testament.

Appendix

Combe Down--- (See page 91).

Combe Down, Bath, so much a focus of attention during my West Country journalistic adventures, continued to keep media representatives on their toes for several years after I had transferred my activities to the east of the country.

The mines stripped of the 'Bath Stone' which went to build a large percentage of the city's buildings, were found to have a mere 6m between the tunnels and the world above and as little as 2m in some places. The mining experts called in to decide what was needed in terms of stabilisation warned that the abandoned workings were likely to collapse in various places threatening life and property. Over the years the mines had been used for a variety of purposes, including a mushroom farm and as an air-raid shelter during the Baedeker raids on Bath in World War ll.

When Bath City Council commissioned studies to survey the condition of the mines they were told they were considered the largest, shallowest and most unstable of their kind in Europe. A boundary was marked out to take into account the safety of 1,660 people living in 760 properties. The area also included a primary school, a nursery and three churches.

Experienced miners were shipped in from South Wales and elsewhere and over a period of 10 years 600.000 cubic metres of foamed concrete were pumped into the underground caverns. The cost was in the region of £166 million and the work was completed in 2011. For the first time for years Combe Downers started to feel safe as the threat of subsidence over a wide area was removed. But even in 2014 there were reminders of what might have happen. Our holiday companions, Frank and Yvonne (never far from some excitement, it seems) woke up one morning in their Combe Down home to find that a part of a lane leading to their front door had subsided. They were still able to get out but only on foot!

Also by John Alexander

Runaway, Red Beret and Reverend   (*ISBN 978-1-78078-017-7)*

Spoofed and Spiked   (*(ISBN 978-07552-1221-7)*